Letters
from the
Caribbean

*To our children, Janey and Ian,
for all their support*

Letters
from the
Caribbean

SAILING IN THE WEST INDIES
Andrea & Ian Treleaven

NEW HOLLAND

Contents

As we said in the introduction to our first book, *Letters from the Med*, you only get one life but plenty of dreams to fulfil. We are still fulfilling ours and our latest has involved selling *Cadiz*, the yacht on which we enjoyed four fantastic cruising seasons in the Mediterranean and wrote about in our book. Our plan was to buy a new one because our next dream was to spend time in the Caribbean and, in the process, sail across the Atlantic as part of the Atlantic Race for Cruisers, a 'to do' box that we've long wanted to tick, all of which would require a yacht that would have to be self-sufficient. And so, despite the fact that the global recession had already started, we sold our Beneteau Oceanis 473 to a fellow Australian and purchased a new Beneteau Oceanis 50 that was delivered direct from the factory in France.

Now, at the end of 2009, we've been lucky enough to spend two glorious seasons in perfect trade wind conditions, returning home to Sydney only when the hurricane season arrived.

About us

For those who haven't read *Letters from the Med*, my husband Ian and I, both Kiwis, have now spent eight cruising seasons in the northern hemisphere after selling our successful Australian-based nautical clothing business – Musto and Line 7 – in 2002.

Ian started his sailing career at the age of seven in Christchurch and grew up to become a vastly experienced yachtsman, while I grew up on a dairy farm in Te Awamutu and was already well into my twenties before my first sailing experience. Interestingly, it was immediately after this that I met Ian at Auckland's Tamaki Yacht Club. Marriage and children – son Ian and daughter

Introduction

Janey – followed along with the establishment of a very successful business, but sailing – including several major races for Ian – has always been a huge part of our family life.

Before I wrote *Letters from the Med*, I'd had no previous experience in writing or photography but since then, with the support of Janey and Ian Jnr, I've written for websites and a number of yachting magazines about our adventures. Photography is now a real passion and we spend many enjoyable evenings on board downloading and editing hundreds of images from the days' activities.

About our yacht

After sailing our Beneteau Oceanis 473 *Cadiz* for four seasons in the Mediterranean we learned what was required for pleasurable cruising over extended periods.

Our new Beneteau Oceanis 50 came with a generator for household power, water-maker, air-conditioning, washing machine, microwave, bow thruster, electric winches, and anchor control from the wheel. The yacht sails on all points exceptionally well, although we try not to sail into the wind but rather follow it. Down below she is very livable with three large sleeping cabins, two separate toilets plus separate stand-up showers and a spacious galley (kitchen) fitted with a fridge and freezer. Especially nice is our large cockpit with a good-sized table, bimini and dodger for shade from the sun. It's out here that we eat and entertain 90 per cent of the time. We've installed an electronic chart plotter in the cockpit for easy navigation and we also have AIS, which identifies approaching ships on the chart on the plotter (see page 45). Serious yachties can read up on the full specs on page 13.

The two Ians – father and son

Daughter Janey

Tips on cruising

As in *Letters from the Med*, throughout the book you will find notes from Ian that cover a range of topics – all of which we hope will make life easier for anyone planning on visiting the region under sail, whether by chartered or private yacht. Please note these tips are not designed to be followed strictly as they merely reflect our own opinions and experience. While it is our aim to encourage others to follow our dream, the number-one rule is to make it easy for everyone, especially one's wife. Otherwise the dream will be over before it starts.

Currency

The euro and US dollar are accepted almost everywhere (although not always at the going bank rate), but it is sometimes necessary to convert to local currencies. France, Spain and the Canaries all use the euro. The Eastern Caribbean Islands use EC$ (Eastern Caribbean dollar) with the exception of the French Islands of Martinique, Guadeloupe, St Barts and St Martin, which use the euro. The Virgin Islands – both US and British – use the US dollar, as does Puerto Rico.

Defining the Caribbean

The Caribbean arc of islands sweeps from Florida to Venezuela separating the Atlantic Ocean and the Caribbean Sea. The larger masses of islands to the north are Cuba, Hispaniola and Puerto Rico, and are known as the Greater Antilles. The Lesser Antilles are made up of the Leeward Islands – from British Virgin Islands to Dominica – and to the south from Martinique to Grenada are the small Windward Islands.

For us, the Caribbean can be summed up as a perfect backdrop of turquoise seas, swaying palms, white sand beaches, blue skies, exotic fish and glorious sunsets. It's also about the art of keeping cool in the tropics.

As for the locals, when we arrived for the first time in Saint Lucia we found their Rastafarian dreadlocks somewhat scary, but we slowly warmed to their laidback style and happy faces. But life is tough for many of them and after we overheard a conversation that included a threat along the lines of 'I could kill you, mon – and I don't need a gun', we soon learned to be conscious of what was going on around us.

Tips on food

I really enjoy cooking in *Cape Finisterre*'s well-appointed galley and as in *Letters from the Med* I've included a number of my favourite recipes (see pages 124–135), tailored for cooking on board and which utilise the mouth-watering tropical fruits that can be found in abundance throughout the islands. We eat a lot of fresh fish but lobster, which is surprisingly cheap, remains our number-one favourite seafood.

Now and again, especially when we are exploring an island, we might treat ourselves to some local fast food such as roti (a wrap filled with curried meat) and jerk chicken (BBQ chicken marinated in a Creole sauce).

My last word on the subject of eating and drinking in the Caribbean is about rum, a drink to which we've become quite partial. We prefer white rum for our cocktails and use a lot of citrus fruit – it's readily available and makes a great mix. Thanks to the presence of so much sugar cane, just about every island in the Caribbean produces its own rum and prices are very competitive averaging out at around AU$15 per litre.

Why we do it

This is now our eighth season cruising in the northern hemisphere and rather than sail back to Australia, as was our original intention in 2003, we have decided to sail back to the Mediterranean where we plan to spend another four seasons.

We enjoy cruising for many reasons, including the way it allows us to meet so many different people.

Andrea and Ian – living the dream

We also love having the company of friends and family on board as well as the opportunity that cruising gives us to visit so many wonderful places including some we might normally never go to, e.g. Cuba and Guatemala.

Most of all we enjoy the freedom of going with the wind and exploring new places away from mainstream tourism. Wherever we are, it's all about getting to know the locals and experiencing different cultures, especially different food and beverages.

Feedback

It is always a pleasure to hear from people who've read *Letters from the Med* and subsequently made the decision to go for it themselves. Thanks to all those who have contacted us with such genuine interest – may your time be spent blue water sailing, enjoying the taste of a cool drink and feeling the sand between your toes.

Setting Off

France–Canary Islands–
Atlantic Crossing

France: A new beginning

It's July 2007 and we've arrived in France via Paris and are on our way down to Les Sables d'Olonne on the Atlantic coast in the Bay of Biscay, north of La Rochelle. We've come here to meet our new yacht and, as if on cue, the hull of our Beneteau Oceanis 50 arrives by truck, taking up the entire road and stopping all traffic. But she's not quite ready for us yet and we have to come back a few days later after she has been commissioned. Contrary to my previous thoughts and needs we are now making life a little easier for ourselves by having a few luxuries installed, including air-conditioning, a water-maker, a washing machine, a microwave and yes, a bow thruster.

This new yacht will be named after Cape Finisterre, the first cape we'll round after leaving the Gulf of Biscay. (The most western point of Europe, Cape Finisterre means 'Land's End' and was so named because hundreds of years ago when explorers sailed off from this cape, they believed the earth to be flat. Hence, in their eyes the land ended at this point.) She is a little bigger than *Cadiz*, our previous yacht, which was our home over several idyllic European summers.

Plans for this year: hopefully we will sail out of here in a week or so and follow the French coast south to San Sebastian just over the border in Spain. We are in no hurry and look forward to this rugged and beautiful coast, famous for its seafood. After Spain we'll sail to Portugal, Gibraltar, Morocco and then out to the Canary Islands where on 25 November we'll set out from Las Palmas on the Atlantic Rally for Cruisers (ARC). Landfall after 2800 nautical miles is the island of St Lucia in the Caribbean. We'll be joined on this race across the Atlantic by our friends Andrew Cochrane, David Lennie, Kevin Horne and Nick and Michelle Smail. Hopefully, after two weeks at sea, we will still all be great friends.

The enormous job of provisioning and ensuring that the safety equipment is satisfactory is finally complete – and I can't help but notice that it's all slowly lowering the waterline. Then on 5 August, the champagne is poured and we officially name our new yacht – and our home for the next 10 months.

Three stubbed toes, a bruised head and the loss of an expensive pair of reading glasses over the side later we are slowly getting used to living on board once again. One might assume that in buying a new yacht everything would be spot on, but no, this has not been the case. At times it's frustrating; very much a trial and error exercise as we get used to the mass of wires behind the cupboards, all necessary to run the various electronics and gadgets on board. Before we leave we must make sure everything is working as once we are down the coast we'll be 'out of sight, out of mind'.

An early test sail when we had to be rescued proved interesting. The starter motor caught on fire and suddenly we were going nowhere. Apart from that incident, we are very happy with how she handled. She is a beautiful yacht.

Ian's Cruising Notes
CAPE FINISTERRE: A BENETEAU OCEANIS 50

Built and launched: 2007

Hull number: 160

Hull construction: solid GRP laminate

Deck construction: balsa sandwich

Length overall: 15.10 metres (50 ft)

Beam (width): 4.49 metres

Draft (depth to bottom of keel): 2.10 metres

Displacement (weight): 13 tonnes (15 tonnes fully loaded)

Cabins: three double (one master, two guest)

Amenities: two heads (toilets) each fitted with a separate stand-up shower

Engine: 110 HP Yanmar

Generator: 5.5kva Onan

Fuel tank capacity: 235 litres diesel (engine 4 litres per hour, generator 1 litre per hour)

Water tank capacity: 565 litres across two tanks

Water-maker: Dessalator 660 duo which operates both 240 volt and 12 volt producing up to 60 litres per hour (depending on the temperature of the sea; the warmer the better)

SAILS

Total area of 115.8 sq metres include:

> Main with lazy jacks and three reefing points
> Roller-furling genoa
> Staysail with hanks for attaching to a
>   removable inner forestay
> 2 gennakers with snuffers

ELECTRONICS

Raymarine E series chart plotter with Raytech version 6 software and Navionics electronic charts

Raymarine ST60 speed, depth, wind direction and speed, depth, water temperature, etc

Raymarine radar

Raymarine cockpit chart plotter

Computer connection at chart table

Raymarine AIS receiver

Raymarine VHF digital radio

Raymarine automatic pilot

Mastervolt battery monitor

TENDER

2.6 metre Bombard with rigid bottom and folding transom and 6HP 2 stroke Yamaha outboard (very lightweight and easy to handle)

La Rochelle

Les Sables-d'Olonne—Biarritz

The morning of our first sail we wake to high winds whistling through the rigging; not what I wanted to hear. I tell myself it sounds worse than it is but there is no holding Ian back. Our first port of call will be La Rochelle, a day sail of 40 nautical miles. It's a good shake down with no problems, only a little bit of excitement when we reach the dock in a strong cross wind, but the bow thruster is proving its worth. The nautical shops in this coastal city soon draw Ian like a bee to a honeypot and I ask myself how he can look at the same things time and time again. Loaded up with lots of bits, he is soon screwing and drilling his heart out.

La Rochelle with its majestic Roman towers at the entrance of the port is an impressive sight. Behind lies a beautiful old stone town that during summer has the air of a carnival with ice-cream parlours everywhere and buskers, street artists and other non-stop entertainment on the street. It's a delight for us to sit with a huge bowl of small sweet black mussels and crusty baguettes to soak up the juices, watching people watching people. But where is summer? Although the weather is settled, it's August and unseasonably cold.

We have decided to follow the coast all the way, ever mindful of the 4-metre tide that changes the coastscape twice a day. Arriving in Royan we tie up to the town wall and admire the wonderful views. Next morning all I can see are the crabs crawling up the wall, because the tide is out (a whole 4 metres!). The port is a delightful trendy beach town where we meet up with Heinz Oser and Christopher, his 10-year-old grandson, for a few days. Crossing the entrance of the Gironde River that leads to Bordeaux, we follow 78 nautical miles of barren coastline to Arcachon. Inland are some of the most

Biarritz

famous vineyards in France: Medoc, Pauillac, St Estephen, St Julien and Margaux to name just a few.

San Sebastian

The sand dunes of Arcachon and its tide-dependent entrance don't make us feel particularly welcome and so we move on to beautiful Biarritz where the golden sand beach is dotted with striped umbrellas and lined with casinos. But we come across some barbecued sardines splashed with thyme vinegar in the fishermen's cove and they are delicious.

Some days are just beautiful and we wouldn't trade places for anything, but then on a bad day it's a different story! We take a risk coming into this corner of the Bay of Biscay as the weather can get very nasty. The prevailing westerly winds are renowned for their ferocity and we are cornered as big seas build from the Atlantic.

After leaving Biarritz we spend our last night in France at anchor in the sheltered bay of St-Jean-de-Luz. It's nice to be able to lower the anchor from the cockpit and know the length dropped without having to run forward, but our luck changes when a windlass problem won't allow us to pull up the anchor the next morning. Totally pissed off, Ian drags me ashore to find a solution to the problem. But because the tide is out we have to scale an iron ladder up the crab-covered seawalls to get to the village. Then we get lucky and find the head sailing instructor. He's very helpful and we are soon on our way.

It is only 25 nautical miles to San Sebastian and we welcome the warmer weather once we sail into Spain. There is no marina at San Sebastian, but there are laid moorings and a very traditional yacht club that welcomes members of recognised yacht clubs. The difference between this Basque part of Spain with its Gothic

The famous tapas bars are what we have come for and we are not disappointed. You pay for what you choose and wash it down with beer or the local cider.

San Sebastian (top left)
Guggenheim, Bilbao (top right)
Tapas for everyone, San Sebastian (bottom)

architecture and France is amazing. The local language is Basque, and very few people speak English. We never realised the strength of the Basque influence until now, especially when we are required to fly the Basque flag from our yacht.

The famous tapas bars are what we have come for and we are not disappointed. Each bar features platters of marinated seafood, peppers and anchovies along with slices of baguette piled high with a variety of toppings including crab mayonnaise, prawns, bacon, egg, etc. You pay for what you choose and wash it down with beer or the local cider, which is not to my liking as it's very bitter and, they warn me, very strong.

It's festival time with lots of fireworks so we enjoy our balmy evening ashore, becoming accustomed to Spanish time. A weather change that night makes us roll as we get side on to the waves that are crashing through the entrance. Trying to sleep is impossible; it's like being in a washing machine! We would like another day here but by the afternoon there are pitching 1-metre-high waves that drive us to explore other options in the bay. Behind the island is a little better, but we are up and down all night checking the tide and trying to prevent other boats from bumping into us.

Enough is enough and we make an early exit to Getaria, a small fishing port with a marina. There we find peace and a good night's sleep. Every village has something to hang its hat on and this one is famous for one of its sons, Juan Sebastian Elcano, who was part of Magellan's expedition that left Spain in September 1519 to sail around the world. Four out of Magellan's five ships did not make it back but Elcano returned as captain of the *Victoria* with just 18 survivors of the voyage on 6 September 1522 – and became known as the first man to have circumnavigated the world.

Bilbao is 50 nautical miles along the coast and by midday we are in the small marina of the Club Maritimo del Abra y Real Sporting Club. We find the metro and visit the Guggenheim Museum in the centre of Bilbao, 20 km up the river. We look

Ian's Cruising Notes
POWER MANAGEMENT

Modern yachts tend to consume a huge amount of power: there's the deep freeze, fridge, computers, television, music (iPod), camera, mobile phone, satellite phone and, when sailing, our navigation gear and auto pilot. However, all our navigation lights are LED, which require very little power.

We installed a 5.5kva generator to charge the batteries and to give us access to 240 volt power when at sea. The yacht came with a 40-amp charger, but this is not sufficient for all the ship's batteries. We left this unit operational to charge the engine and generator batteries and had an extra 80-amp charger installed to charge the 4 x 140-amp hr house batteries. We are increasing them next season to 4 x 200-amp hr batteries. Also installed was a Mastervolt battery monitor which displays charge, input and output of each battery bank.

When at anchor we only have to charge for three hours once a day using three litres of diesel. As it is producing 240 volts we take the opportunity to either make water from the desalinator at 50 litres per hour or run our washing machine to maximise use of the generator. At sea, we run the genset for 2½ hours twice a day.

down past the old Spanish apartments at this world-renowned modern art museum with its titanium 'fish scales' glistening in the sun and say, 'Wow!' The design depicts Bilbao's ancient fishing heritage using boats and fish in a stylised way, not unlike the Sydney Opera House.

We attempt to leave for La Coruna but after motoring out to the breakwater we find the breaking seas and wind direction not to our liking, especially when we couldn't see the top of the masts of the yachts beside us amid the large waves. Deciding to wait for another day, we return to the shelter of the yacht club.

The Roman-built 'Tower of Hercules' lighthouse, La Coruna

Bilbao–La Coruna

Our stay in Bilbao lasted for six days and many times over this period it crossed our minds that maybe we had made a mistake by coming along this coast rather than taking the shortcut across the Bay of Biscay.

Eventually though, kitted out in wet weather gear, safety harnesses and life jackets, it's the right time to go. With 30-knot winds, we sail wing and wing (i.e. the wind is directly behind us so the mainsail is on the opposite side to the headsail) roller-coasting our way down the waves for 70 nautical miles. There's no stopping Ian, but I'm shit scared alone in the cockpit while Ian's down below fixing something or other. He loves this stuff, as do all yachtsmen, but my nerves are shattered. But we make it to Ribadeo, in less than 3 hours, averaging 8.5 knots entering between breaking sandbanks, lining up bridges, church steeples and leading marks.

It feels good to have rounded the top of this continent and be heading south. Then the boom comes down ... what is it with Ian and booms? One nut falls to the deck and that's the end of sailing, good company and whatever we had planned for that day. But on our arrival in La Coruna that first warm breeze across our faces lifts our spirits.

La Coruna, rounding Cape Finisterre–Vigo

At the entrance to La Coruna is the Roman-built 'Tower of Hercules' lighthouse, reputedly the oldest working lighthouse in the world, but little remains of the original structure. Our overall impression is of a Modernist city of glass, wrought iron and stone. We stay for three days, anchored in the bay, enjoying the evening concerts in the square and several good restaurants.

At one in particular we order pimientos (the local peppers), which, in our experience, are not usually that hot, but unfortunately Ian gets a hot one. The next day, with his rear end on fire, he declares he will not be eating any more of them.

The boom is now temporarily repaired and Janey, our daughter, arrives in time to sail with us around Cape Finisterre, the westernmost point of Europe, once known as the end of the world, as mentioned earlier, and after which we have named our boat. At the Cape there is no welcoming party, just hundreds of seagulls excited to see us. Finisterre itself is a small fishing port where we have a seafood lunch of cockles, razor horns, squid and wine to toast our own *Cape Finisterre*.

All along the coast are *rias*, the Spanish word for estuaries or inlets. They're very beautiful with their white beaches and contrasting green pine trees. They are also a navigation nightmare full of clam and mussel fish farms. Just when I'm starting to wonder what the hell we are doing here, we have the most fantastic day in Santiago de Compostela, 30 km inland from the nearest port of Vilagarcia. The story goes that Saint James, one of Christ's disciples, was beheaded, put in a stone boat and ended up here in the Ria de Arosa (a flooded river valley that is now a firth) before being taken inland. Over a number of centuries this route has become a pilgrims' walk with the famous Santiago de Compostela cathedral built of granite back in the ninth century being the destination. So many pilgrims have laid their hands on the pillar just inside the doorway that a groove has been worn in the stone.

After visiting the cathedral we walk down the narrow laneways full of restaurants offering an amazing degustation of fresh scallops, prawns, cockles and sardines just waiting to be cooked. The tapas bars are laden with equally tantalising titbits such as toasted bread topped with tuna, salami, or grilled peppers – presided over by welcoming hosts.

We spend a day anchored off a beach near Vigo, the sky is blue, the weather settled and yes, it's warm enough to swim.

Port of Finisterre

Santiago de Compostela cathedral

Port of Combarro, Spain (top left and right)   *Bayona (top right), Porto (bottom right)*

Vigo, Spain—Porto, Portugal

Our last port in Spain before Portugal is Baiona. Ian was here as a 24-year-old on a 52-ft yacht named *Congere* and all he could remember of that time was that the bar was in a castle. Back then *Congere* was a competitor in the 1972 transatlantic yacht race from Bermuda to Baiona. Known as the 'Race of Rediscovery', it was organised to commemorate the anniversary of the return of *Pinta* in 1493 from the Americas to announce Columbus' discovery of the new lands.

Soon enough it is time to head south to Portugal – with not a lot of wind around. Porto, or the Douro River, has no marina so we are advised to stay 5 nautical miles north at Leixos. Authority in the form of customs agents and the police along with representatives from the port authority descend on us the moment we

arrive. We take a train from the marina and later stand on the bridge high above Porto, which looks stunning on this clear blue day. Below on the left bank are the 'Houses of Port Wine' with their attractive terracotta roofs; it's in these houses that the port is stored for many years. On the right bank is the very colourful old town; steeples and history everywhere. It's not an easy place to get around as the steep streets are cobbled, making it difficult to walk. But we navigate ourselves to the source of Taylor's Port; first on Ian's list and then cobble our way back up the hill for lunch at Taylor's restaurant, Barao de Fladgate, with its delicious menu. Port is served as an aperitif, then we have to choose between king prawns with a port mayonnaise, duck with port raspberries or steak with port wine sauce.

The next day our five-hour round train trip takes us along the Upper Douro River to Pinhao, taking in some

MÃ OS À OBRA!
JUNTOS NO PROJECTO DE RECUPERAÇÃO DO PALÁCIO DA BOLSA.

Pena Palace, Sintra

spectacular scenery. Hillside after hillside is terraced, sometimes very steeply, running at all angles. The rock is so hard in this part of Portugal that they have to blast it before planting vines, which then have to grow down until they find water for themselves. Very hot in summer and bitterly cold in winter, the region is famous for its port grapes that are picked at the end of each September; we are amazed to learn that in this day and age the grapes are still squashed by foot; we're told it's still the kindest way to extract the juice for vintage port. Apparently they are trodden for 24 hours and when the fermenting starts the workers dance to folk music.

After three days in a port, just when I have worked out how to get around, where to buy an electronic train ticket, which shop sells the best bread and where to find a tourism office, it's time to leave, only to start all over again in the next port.

In the meantime, though, this is the notoriously exposed Atlantic coast of Portugal and what do we get? Fog, flat glassy seas and no wind. And what do you do while motoring for 12 hours? You watch for craypots, whip rope ends, photograph the occasional bird and write letters. Next stop is Nazare, one of the most famous fishing towns in Portugal, and would you believe it – police, immigration, customs and port authorities all over again!

Lisbon

Before entering Lisbon up the Rio Tejo we stop at Cascais, the holiday port that has grown from being a small fishing village to the stylish place it is today. We're absolutely loving Portugal so far – everyone speaks English and they are all so extremely pleasant and

helpful. The marina has good facilities and tradesmen so Ian takes the opportunity to get some repairs done, which means a lot of our time gets taken up with workmen coming and going.

We go to visit Palacio da Pena or Pena Palace high up in Sintra, once a royal town. Set above the village in a landscape of planted trees, the grounds of the palace cover 200 acres. On this very hot day the coolness under the trees is very welcoming as we wind our way up to the pastel-coloured Disney-like castle. The turrets, towers, terraces and other details are an interesting mix of styles, and the interior hasn't changed since its last royal occupant, Queen Amelia, left in 1910.

Then it's up the river to Lisbon and Marina Alcantara, which is close to the city centre (but getting the tide right is important; against us is 3 knots). We pass the impressive Discoveries Monument, erected in 1960 to commemorate the death 500 years before of Prince Henry the Navigator.

We leave Lisbon with a wonderful memory of a balmy evening spent aboard an old wooden tram. As we rattle through this multicultural city (full of African, Indian, and Portuguese ethnicities), tram window down, we watch aspects of history pass by. Castles, churches, museums – Lisbon has them all, especially the Maritime Museum, which is one of the best we have ever visited; its collection includes over 17,000 items, 30,000 photographs as well as original plans and archives of approximately 1500 ships.

Later our own navigating takes us round Cabo de Sao Vicente on the southwest corner and we are now heading east along the Algarve coast with very little wind and no sign of the 'ever present' swell that we've read about.

Note from Ian: Andrea is very good at telling you what I do wrong so now it is my turn. On one particular occasion the outboard had been difficult to start and on investigation I discovered that she had been sold *petro* (degreaser) instead of petrol. It's amazing that the engine still ran, albeit on one cylinder.

Ian's Cruising Notes
COMMUNICATIONS

We chose to install an Iridium satellite phone instead of the traditional SSB long-distance radio, mostly because we have never been 'chatterers' and it gives us better emergency access. This phone also has internet and email access, which we used for sending emails and even small photo images when we were crossing the Atlantic and again in Cuba where internet facilities are limited, and has the added advantage of a built-in tracker that plots our position on our website once a day or as often as we require it. This last feature makes leaving the yacht for a few days (or during the off-season) less risky because we can log on at any time to check that it (the yacht) hasn't moved.

We also have digital VHF radio which keeps us in touch with any nearby vessels and while in port it allows us to listen to the daily cruising net organised by fellow yachties. Using the MMSI (Maritime Mobile Service Identity) we can communicate directly with other ships and yachts without people listening in (to obtain your own MMSI registration your yacht must be registered in your country of origin and you must have a radio operator's licence).

Lisbon Mall (top)
Prince Henry the Navigator's
School of Navigation and
lighthouse (middle)
Southern Portugal (bottom)

Rugged coastline near Faro, Portugal

Cabo de Sao Vicente, Portugal –Cadiz, Spain

Rounding Cabo de Sao Vicente, the southernmost part of Portugal, is a different experience altogether. It's hot; the sea is blue and lined with cliffs of golden sandstone that have been carved into many shapes by the Atlantic. High on a barren exposed cliff is what's left of Prince Henry the Navigator's School of Navigation, founded in the fifteenth century, but not a lot remains.

So far fishing has just not been our thing; after catching nothing we've now resorted to spending big on a flashy metallic rod, reel and bright shiny lures so we're very excited once our rod holder is screwed on and out goes the copper-coloured line. The sails are up on this beautiful day and would you believe it? The first thing we catch is a craypot buoy. Ian doesn't want to lose his new lure so off he goes in the dinghy to cut it free, but then a

little wind gets into the sail and the next thing I hear is an awful yell from Ian to release the fishing line because he's got the hook in his thumb and I am now towing him along with the dinghy and craypot. Ian survived the experience but the craypot didn't. Discovering the town of Mateus in Portugal reminded us baby boomers of the days when we used to drink Mateus rosé wine. For old time's sake we buy a bottle – it's also useful for deadening the pain in Ian's thumb. Our tastes must have changed though, and we decide that the unusual bottle is only good for sticking a candle in it and letting the wax drip over the sides or perhaps topping it with a lampshade.

When we near Cadiz, in Spain, after a beautiful all-day sail of 85 nautical miles it feels like we are coming home as we enter the bay. (Still no tuna caught on the new line!) Five years ago we left this place in our other yacht, *Cadiz*, not knowing what the future would hold. El Puerto de

Going ashore near Faro

Santa Maria, Cadiz

The Alcazar, Seville

Santa Maria Royal Yacht Club is our base for the next three days and it's so hot that the air-conditioning has to run on full.

El Puerto de Santa Maria is famous for its bullring, its sherry and the fact that Christopher Columbus left from here to discover America. First stop for us is at the sherry producers Gutierrez-Colosia where we learn about the history and tradition of sherry and the region. Needless to say, we come away with a bottle or two.

Then it's off to Seville by train for the day and although we practically melt in the 35°C heat, we take in the Gothic cathedral of Seville (also known as Catedral de Santa Maria de la Sede), La Giralda (its bell tower) and the Alcazar (a palace constructed in the twelfth century). The tomb of Christopher Columbus is in the cathedral but DNA has recently proved it is not Columbus; and he is supposedly buried in the Caribbean. The Islamic influence in design and colour in this city is very much present.

Approaching Gibraltar

Cadiz, Spain—Mohammedia, Morocco

On a calm and clear blue day we sail past Cape Trafalgar. Rounding Tarifa Point we can see North Africa only 10 miles away; it seems so close we could reach out and grab it. So far we have sailed 1400 nautical miles from Les Sables-d'Olonne in France to Gibraltar, the southernmost tip of our European Atlantic coastal trip this year.

Gibraltar offers us not much more than some rain, fish and chips for lunch, and a televised rugby game in the Lord Nelson bar. We decide that one day here is enough. It's changed into a development site, it's no longer easy to have work done on our boat and the chandlery shops are almost non-existent.

The weather is perfect so we go down memory lane and cruise 50 nautical miles into the Mediterranean along the Costa del Sol as far east as Malaga. It's been five years since we were last here and in that time the prices have more than doubled in the marinas (Puerto Banus now 130 Euro per night), it's harder to get a berth and the number of resorts and high-rise apartments along the seaside have multiplied.

At Marbella Marina we are joined by John and Andrea Connolly. Dodging all the ships, we cross the shipping lanes to North Africa. Morocco, here we come!

Morocco

We don't exactly blend in on our arrival in the port of Tangier. After four hours spent crossing the strait, we are all very excited and wonder just how different it will be here. As we motor past the numerous colourful fishing boats we notice hundreds of men and boys lining the sides of the fishing port waiting for work. When we get to the marina, with the old medina rising up in front of us and the sounds of the minaret ringing out, it's full, so rafting up is the only option.

We haven't even finished mooring and already the touts are here offering their services as guides. Customs and police visit for check-in, a procedure that takes place at every port in Morocco. By the time we navigate our way into the medina, past all the pestering men touting their services and into the market, we feel shell-shocked.

It's one hour before 6 pm during Ramadan, which is probably not the best time to be here as fasting all day and eating through the night makes the local men grumpy. A frenzy of people, mostly men, surround us everywhere we go and we are not made welcome. I go to buy bread and they won't serve me; they will only take an order from Ian. As we enter the souk, we're overcome by feelings of claustrophobia. The smells of raw meat, spices and olives are enough to cut the air. As soon as possible we take refuge in an international hotel where we are welcomed and the beer soon starts to flow. By the time we get back to the comfort of *Cape Finisterre* we feel more than a little bewildered and decide on a peaceful barbecue dinner at the back of the yacht.

Next day we arrange a tour guide and enjoy a drive through the affluent green areas overlooking the medina which we view through palms, bougainvillea and picturesque white arches. But we are soon back in the madness, which on the one hand is fascinating but on the other keeps us alert and on guard. Taking photos is difficult; nearly every time I try I get thumped on the back or given the 'evil eye' sign.

We are happy to leave and are soon rounding Cap Spartel lighthouse where the Mediterranean Sea meets the Atlantic, causing the two currents to overflow.

Asilah, originally a Phoenician port with a fifteenth-century fortified medina built by the Portuguese, is our next stop. Ours is the only yacht to anchor here for the night and there are facilities only for the fishermen. Going in at high tide knowing we have only just enough water under us at low tide with nowhere else to go is a little worrying. Ashore, behind a high stone wall, we find a clean white medina. Attractive blue doors, hanging bougainvillea and the usual colourful (but useless to us) souvenirs catch our eye.

Zakaria, who befriended us while moored alongside our boat in Tangier, is also here and he shows us around. It's so good to talk to an educated Moroccan; we gain a better understanding of the place after his explanation of the Muslim faith and related lifestyle. Not a lot appears to have changed in the last thousand years.

What excitement when Ian and John catch the first fish! Under full sail we motor backwards when it happens,

Next day we arrange a tour guide and enjoy a drive through the affluent green areas overlooking the Medina which we view through palms, bougainvillea and picturesque white arches.

Buying bread in the market   Asilah

Scenes from Casablanca (right)

thinking we had once again hooked a piece of rubbish. Then we see this beautiful big yellow and green fish. Pity we have to kill it (the winch handle comes in handy at this point), and we end up with blood everywhere. But now we have eaten it I have to say it's the best piece of fish I've had in a long time.

After a very long day at sea approaching Mohammedia (a port city 15 miles northeast of Casablanca) at night we are confused by a strong and continuous red light. One minute it seems as if it is very close and we alter course thinking it's a boat. For 16 miles it baffles us and it's not until the next day while we are visiting the Hassan 11 Mosque in Casablanca that we learn it's actually a laser beam shining east towards Mecca. A bit confusing for the likes of us but we need to be constantly on the lookout due to so many fishing boats without lights and charted shore beacons that are not working.

Mohammedia, Casablanca, Fez, Marrakesh

We decide to tie up at the marina in Mohammedia, the only one on this coast, as the new marina being built in Casablanca will not be complete for another couple of years. Mohammedia Marina is also well guarded (the King's personal launch is in view of our berth), making it a good place from which to visit all the places we want to see.

The romance of Casablanca has most of us dreaming about it but at last we are here. A 'petit taxi' takes us to the edge of town, then a 'grand taxi' to Casablanca itself. There's nothing grand about either vehicle – no air-conditioning and no handles for the windows unless you ask the driver in which case he passes you one. We are not very impressed by the poverty we see on the way and negotiate for the taxi to stay with us while we look around. Eventually we get to the vast and very grand

The Medina, Fez (top)
Riad, Fez (bottom)

Hassan 11 Mosque, the construction of which began in 1986 and was completed in 1993, four years after King Hassan 11's 60th birthday, the original completion date. Built on the waterfront on the site of a shantytown, it's one of the very few mosques in the world that allow non-Muslims inside. Most of the materials used for the building of the mosque are local but some, such as the glass chandeliers and granite columns, were imported. The 200-metre-high minaret looks over a city in which one-third of its population lives without sewerage, so a lot of this excessive show doesn't make sense to us. However, from the washing fountains to the steam rooms it's all very impressive to look at.

Next day a five-hour train trip takes us all inland to the medieval city of Fez where we plan to stay overnight. It's high season and accommodation isn't easy to find, particularly as we have our hearts set on staying in a riad, a traditional Moroccan house or palace with an interior garden (the word riad comes from the Arabian term for garden, 'ryad'). We're successful though and are met outside the medina by the manager of the riad who directs us down a series of narrow lanes with very high walls made of Sahara clay plaster, engulfing us in another world.

A large key produced by the manager unlocks a carved wooden door in the shape of an arch and we gasp as we enter. The interior of high white-plastered walls, inset with tiles of blue and white and carved wood, with gold inlay ceilings, represents for us the colours of Morocco – the colours we have come to see. We relax and sip mint tea, gazing out to the private garden of arches covered in jasmine that give the riad its name: Au vingt Jasmins (which translates as 20 Jasmines).

After an alcohol-free lunch we take a guided tour through the maze of streets but all the boys are looking for is a cold beer. Along an alleyway near our hotel is Riad Fes, a spectacular hotel with a superb modern Moroccan interior. It offers a world-class bar and restaurant in which we comfortably install ourselves and we couldn't be happier.

Andrea and John are great company but they need to return to Spain. We return to our yacht very satisfied

Admiring carpets in the Souk, Marrakesh

with our new perspective on Morocco. Kevin Horne is about to join us and on his arrival we'll head straight to the Canary Islands, a 430-nautical-mile crossing to Lanzarote, the easternmost of the islands.

Getting fuel is something of an experience for us as we have to carry our empty 30-litre jerry cans to the fuel station about 1 km away and then carry them back once they've been filled. Only four weeks to go before the race across the Atlantic – every time I think about it I get a shivery feeling in my stomach.

For Ian's 60th birthday we go inland to Marrakesh aboard the Marrakesh Express. Our destination is a special place on the edge of the Atlas Mountains and the Sahara Desert. An oasis of tall palm trees greets us after our train ride through the desert and we're soon in the middle of a complex of pink stucco buildings that make up the medina with its 15 arched entrances.

There appear to be noisy mopeds by the hundreds and we gradually adjust to the shock of seeing Berbers and Arabs living as they have done for hundreds of years.

Riad Farnatchi where we are staying is inside the manic medina, complete with its own private hammam (spa). It's authentic but luxurious and the central courtyard with its pool and the sounds of running water over which rooms with their own balconies look down is very cooling. I spend the afternoon relaxing after a black soap scrub on hot white marble tiles in the hammam. The nicest thing about these places is the calming effect they have on you.

The medina's souk is a pleasant and colourful surprise of carpets, silverware and pyramids of sweet cakes as we pass through on our way to the Djemaa el Fna Square. Here we spend an evening like no other we've ever experienced. Snake charmers, storytellers, acrobats and

Graciosa, Canary Islands

fortune-tellers entertain the crowds, which are made up of locals rather than tourists. Around the square are food stalls offering sheep's head stew, snail soup and fried fish among other delicacies. We sit down on the benches provided and enjoy the atmosphere.

Mohammedia, Morocco– Graciosa, Canary Islands

A dream run south to the 29th latitude, 1700 miles north of the equator and where it is summer all year round. My first impression of the northernmost Canary Islands is that they are similar to the Kornati Islands in Croatia, flat barren sand dunes, with evidence of volcanic eruptions scattered over the landscape.

The island of Graciosa is our landfall and as we enter between two islands a local wind hits us at 40 knots. After securing our boat to a fishing vessel Ian ventures ashore to the village where sand swirls through the streets; it is straight out of a western movie. We organise to drive around the island in a Land Rover, which takes just one hour. Kevin says that throughout the drive his head was filled with the theme music from *The Good, the Bad and the Ugly.*

We soon find a bay, Playa Francesa, in which to anchor for a few days. The water is crystal clear and we enjoy being able to swim again during the day after being in Morocco. Another day is spent climbing the volcano to see the panoramic views of spectacular black cliffs – it's exercise we all need.

Lanzarote Island

It's a boy's day with a fast sail down the coast. As we enter the cosy port of Arrecife, the capital of Lanzarote, we spot New Zealanders, plus English and Swedish

Home of Cesar Manrique, Lanzarote

Fuerteventura

people all cruising in different directions. The port is full of half-submerged boats that are going nowhere anytime soon and I can only assume they have been confiscated from captured Moroccan refugees. It's a constant reminder that refugees should not be approached along this coast, as it is so close to Africa.

Marina Puerto Calero, the Puerto Cervo of the Canary Islands, is modern and purpose-built for regattas. It is home to us for a few days and it's here that Ian slowly recovers from gastroenteritis, a souvenir from Morocco that he picked up when he had to untangle our anchor with his bare hands in the mud (and probably a lot of raw sewage) on the bottom of the bay. He actually ends up in the emergency department of the hospital in Lanzarote. The first thing he says to me when he wakes up there is 'Are you poisoning me?'

In 1730 this island burst into a series of eruptions that lasted for six years, leaving a land of black lava with many cone-shaped mountains. Today, thanks to the late Cesar Manrique, an artist, the island has a lot of style and interesting features. Realising the potential influence of tourism, Manrique could see the importance of keeping the island looking as natural as possible. No building is over two storeys high, they're all flat-roofed and painted white. You won't find a blade of grass anywhere; the gardens are filled with cactus and other plants that need very little water. During our stay we are told it hasn't rained here for a year and the vineyards in the centre of the island are suffering. We have never seen anything like it and stop for lunch at one of the inland vineyards, el Chupadero, where we feel volcanic stones beneath our feet and taste delicious tapas. The owner of the bodega (winery) explains that although the vines are very low in profile they produce an enormous number of grapes. The moisture that keeps the vines alive comes from the overnight dew. We try a local drop, a white Malvasia, which is very dry and very drinkable.

Open to the public, Cesar Manrique's home and artistic creation is very inspiring. Set inland on a black lava flow it comprises a two-storey white house with five large 'bubbles' connected by tunnels. These days the bubbles are sitting rooms or cactus gardens complete with turquoise pool. Looking out a large window all we

can see are ripples of black lava and in the distance a volcanic cone mountain.

We enjoy anchoring and swimming in crystal-clear seas under endless blue skies, but does it ever rain here?

Meanwhile, we rename our yacht 'The Money Drain'; every port we visit we seem to spend more time and money on preparing for the ARC. Ideas get tested at sea and are then modified on shore.

Las Palmas—Gran Canaria

We arrive at Las Palmas where the Atlantic Rally for Cruisers race to the Caribbean will start on 25 November. So far the winds have been very light but with just 14 days to go that could change. On board preparations for the two weeks we'll be at sea are now top priority, along with lots of social activity.

Two thousand and forty-five nautical miles behind us and, as Ian likes to remind me, 2800 nautical miles to go to get across the Atlantic.

Keith and Caryl Turner from Wellington, New Zealand, have us fascinated by their story of cruising for the past three years. They bought a yacht in the USA and sailed across the Atlantic to the Med with not a lot of experience but they now have a wealth of knowledge under their respective belts and are finally about to sail home to New Zealand. Great to see people living their dream!

Our marina – home for the next two weeks – is full to capacity with 245 yachts entered for the race. Officially the event is a rally, but when does a rally become a race? Just this morning the race director told us to enjoy the start, hang back and take some photos; there are 20 days to go. I look at Ian's face and see that the director's comment has gone completely over his racing head. As for the photos, I should be so lucky. From maxi-yachts and catamarans, down to small cruising yachts old and new, it is looking like one big boat show.

As our crew arrives, comprising four New Zealanders and three Australians: Nick and Michelle Smail, Kevin Horne, Andrew Cochrane, David Lennie and of course Ian and myself, we look forward to an exciting build-up to the race.

They are about to turn my home into a racing yacht.

Our marina — home for the next two weeks — is full to capacity with 245 yachts entered for the race. Officially the event is a rally, but when does a rally become a race?

ARC 2007 Las Palmas, Gran Canaria–St Lucia, Caribbean

We elect to become part of the ARC, which always starts on the last Sunday of November just as the trade winds from the east are setting in for the season, for our crossing. It's a well-organised event both socially and safety-wise and it will be nice for us to sail in company.

This prestigious event has been running for over 30 years and attracts up to 240 entrants. The work involved in making our yacht safe will stand us in good stead for our future cruising plans. (It's probably also worth mentioning the other reason for choosing to join the rally, which is Ian's competitive streak; he can't wait to sail against so many other yachts!)

As mentioned earlier there are seven of us on board. I'm feeling a kind of nervous excitement about the trip: two-plus weeks at sea with no chance to turn back and the possibility of being seasick. At one point I actually considered flying, but at the back of my mind I couldn't help but think about how I'd feel if they ended up having a great trip and I'd missed out on this once-in-a-lifetime experience.

With 1200 crew including children, the event is quite a challenge for the ARC organisers. And while the ceremonies, parties, flag parades, seminars, etc are all very exciting and informative, once you're at the start line it's just you and the Atlantic. The sea can never be taken for granted; we've learned to always expect the unexpected and to plan for every eventuality.

Late to fill in, the trade winds are perfect for the 200 yachts in the cruising division on the start line. There's a 25-knot northerly predicted and it should stay that way for five days. The sea temperature here is 20°C and is expected to be 26°C at our destination, so the odd little wave across the bow will be welcome.

Provisioning

The provisioning of a yacht for an Atlantic crossing requires a day-by-day menu plan. It's not to be taken lightly because once the boat leaves the dock it becomes a floating supermarket that in our case has to cater for seven people for up to 16 days, plus hold

Ian's Cruising Notes

There's a wonderful festive atmosphere to the lead-up in Las Palmas. Daily activities include well-organised seminars on safety and efficiency plus great social events allowing everyone to meet their fellow competitors. Safety requirements are very stringent (almost up to Sydney to Hobart Race standards) and each entrant is inspected and signed off. It is a great discipline for ensuring all vessels have all correct safety equipment on board including emergency steering and a permanently mounted back-up navigation light system.

Once we're under way each yacht has to email their position daily at 1200 hrs as there are too many yachts to operate a radio schedule. The inbuilt tracker on our iridium phone reports our position to the race office on time each day but we also email our position as back-up.

For the crossing the Australian contingent of five yachts engage a weather router to assist with our track. We report our position to him twice a day and he returns a new waypoint to head for to maximise the weather and speed. We finish 23rd across the line beating many larger yachts and attribute a large part of this fantastic result to his advice.

something in reserve for an emergency. Stowage must be well planned, too, because the fridge and freezer are relatively small and not all the fresh fruit and vegetables will last the distance.

Another important issue is easy access, but here Ian came up with the brilliant idea of dividing our non-perishable food items into four-day 'rations', i.e. four separate boxes each containing a range of goodies. This way the favourite chocolate biscuits will not all get eaten on the first day plus we won't have the problem of 'where did we stow that?'

Before we leave Michelle and I cook and freeze six separate meals – it is one of the best things we ever do. Apart from the convenience we are able to dispose of a lot of rubbish in advance and we can also include

Getting shipshape (top, right and bottom right)

vegetables in the meals that might not have otherwise been possible given our storage issues. Speaking of rubbish, we're very careful about keeping on board all non-biodegradable items. We might not be a pretty sight on our arrival in St Lucia what with all the black bags hanging off the stern, but we think it's worth the effort.

Water

If we have to, we can survive on water alone. Our Beneteau Oceanis 50 has the capacity to carry 550 litres of water in two separate tanks, but we also have a water-maker on board (although one thing we've learned is that all these optional 'add-ons' break down with monotonous regularity). Our second tank we will keep full at all times (we'll only use it in an emergency), and we'll top up our other tank as we go.

sailing under spinnaker

We prefer bottled water for drinking and at the start of every day each crew member will be given a 1.5-litre bottle, labelled with their name, with strict instructions to drink it all because dehydration can cause many problems.

First aid

Before we leave France our friend Dr Heinz Oser arranges for us a simple but comprehensive medical kit. Apart from the usual antibiotics, Band-Aids and suppositories for seasickness, we also carry a range from local anaesthetic, needles and sutures to temporary tooth fillings. It could be a never-ending list but the main thing is to be able to stop any bleeding, treat burns and administer pain relief when necessary. Some of us have also completed a first-aid course but as there are 40 doctors participating in the race, help will never be too far away.

Safety

The advantage of participating in an official rally such as the ARC is that it encourages everyone to get their yacht up to standard safety-wise and ensure that all on board fittings and equipment work the way they are supposed to. Ian doesn't have to rewrite the safety rules as we are given a very comprehensive manual – the best he has seen – before the race starts. We plan a training day for all the crew in which everyone is given a role in case of a 'man overboard' or 'abandon ship' scenario. In addition to the survival 'grab bag' we always have in place, we make up another waterproof bag containing all passports, credit cards plus some cash so that we will be prepared in the event that we end up in an unexpected place.

The start

All yachts are requested to fly the decorative international code flags, making for a spectacular sight across the marina. Here from Sydney are John and Sue Gilder on *Story Teller*, John and Irene Hunt on *Southern Princess*, Phil and Robbie Hearse on *Anteater Blues*, and from Brisbane Hans and Suzanne Pettersson on *Mullee Mullee*.

We are promised downwind sailing for this race to the Caribbean and that's exactly what we get. The start is a fresh northerly as two start lines get the gun for a south course down the east side of Gran Canaria Island. First off is the racing division of 35 yachts and then, 20 minutes later, it's our start in the cruising division. Gennaker up, we soon leave the fleet in our wake as most yachts make a conservative start without a gennaker flying.

Sailing at 10+ knots and reaching speeds of 18 knots with the help of rain squalls and big waves, we are flying. All I have to do is hold on! There are two routes we can take: a direct line to St Lucia or a more southerly route towards the Cape Verde Islands, turning left 'when the butter melts' and running with the trade winds. We are taking the second option but cut the corner slightly as

our weatherman predicts there will be enough wind to cut through the wind shadow of the Canary Islands (this wind shadow can extend out for over 150 nautical miles).

Along with the other Australian yachts we share the services of Australian weatherman Bruce Buckley. We email him our position on a daily basis and he responds with the most favourable course to follow – all the while he's sitting at home in Perth.

By evening there's not another yacht in sight and we settle down to running with a 4-metre swell. The islands cast a shadow over the southern point and we have some light winds overnight. With the gennaker up for 24 hours we cover 193 nautical miles and suddenly it's not a rally, but a race, with the boys on board revelling in the conditions.

We email the first schedule for yacht positions at midday and we are pleased to learn from the list received later in the day that we are in a very favourable southerly position relative to other yachts of interest to us.

The ARC crew

My daily diary

Day 2. The first 24 hours are the hardest and most of us are tired so we take advantage of our off-watch time to sleep. Two other race yachts sighted during the day turn out to be 90+ footers. Gennaker still flying until night falls when the tack ring rips off and away she flies. The next hour is spent sewing webbing to sail – and the odd finger. Not a very easy job but up she went again and fingers crossed it will last the distance.

Day 3. Catching a huge dorado fish fills in the morning. We move southwest at 7 knots in flat calm seas and a beautiful blue sky. Sashimi for lunch thanks to having come prepared with wasabi, soy sauce and homemade pickled ginger.

It is fantastic to have an iridium satellite telephone on board and email access to weather and all yacht positions. Reality is hitting in as to how long we are going to be out here.

Ian calls this 'Champagne Sailing' but I wouldn't go that far! With beautiful downhill sailing during the day, we have our moments with unpredictable squalls going through in the evenings. We can see from ARC reports that we are doing quite well but it's still early days and a no-wind area is ahead of us. Our first report received puts us in 32nd position boat for boat in the whole fleet of 240 yachts, including racing and maxi division.

Day 4. Settling into a routine but hate getting up in the night; I can't see a thing, power is precious, so much to put on ... wet weather gear, harness and personal EPIRB (emergency position-indicating radio beacon). It's compulsory for all yachts to have one of these but we also choose to have personal units in the event of any of us falling in the water. Each beacon has a serial number that is registered with the national authority of the country the yacht is registered in – in our case Australia. The Australian Marine Safety Authority (AMSA) has all our emergency contacts in case any of the EPIRBs registered to our yacht are activated. Our son and daughter always know approximately where we are.

During the night we have a three-hourly watch change and during the day four-hourly. Michelle and I are very grateful for all the precooked meals; we still seem to be very busy during our watch. With 18 knots of wind and the gennaker still flying, the boys also have their hands full and love it. Even with everything going on we still have time to get out the fishing line and it's not long before we pull in the big one. A 12-kg beautiful yellow dorado is on the BBQ an hour later and there's enough fish left over to put in the freezer. No more fishing for us as we will only take from the sea what we can eat.

Day 5. The yachts taking the northerly rhumb line route (a straight line between departure and destination points) are leading, but our weatherman assures us the middle route is the best long-term proposition for better trade winds.

Day 6. Golden sunrise, clear to the horizon, dolphins and yet I'm feeling very lonely in this big blue ocean. Trade winds are consistent at 16 knots and we average 9.5 knots all day to achieve our 200 miles in 24 hours.

This morning we are in 13th place, boat for boat, out of the whole fleet, so it's no wonder we haven't seen another yacht for two days. We are first in our division. Can't believe it!

Before we left we were warned to report – and stay clear of – any refugees. An ARC participant gets too close to one such boat and two refugees swim to the yacht. The crew secure their unexpected visitors and have to stand by until a police helicopter arrives. And on a Volvo 60 a crewman is badly burned after a broach and is taken off by a ship. Two reminders to be very careful!

Day 7. Reaching the 1000 nautical miles mark, we have 1800 to go. With very dark nights, we run wing-and-wing with our headsail poled out, getting a better heading and have a no-stress night for a change. It is very important to preserve our spinnakers as we have had to repair them on several occasions. Good winds all day reaching 22 knots, 3-metre seas and lots of flying fish.

Ian is very impressed with the performance of our yacht, she runs beautifully and life down below is very comfortable; we don't feel the speeds we are achieving on deck.

Andrew talks of ice-cream and passionfruit, Michelle has adapted her yoga positions to suit the cabin and I keep my eye on the destination date, which is shown on the computer screen calculated by our current speed. I have to say it is a wonderful sail and considering the rolling seas we are on an even keel. From here on we are on a slide to St Lucia. Time to destination is getting longer as very little wind is around. Having adapted to balancing to the yacht's motion, we now find ourselves almost becalmed with flat seas, stuck between two weather systems.

Day 8. Today we are holding onto a 16-knot SE as we slice through the 3-metre seas, heading west. Air temperature of 30°C for most of the day and rain is predicted, but very pleasant sailing although muggy in the saloon. Even the seawater temperature is up to 23 degrees and we'd love a swim, but that's impossible. No stopping the boys now!

A Mayday is dispatched by a non-ARC participant and a race yacht goes to their aid. Finding them in their life raft and yacht still afloat, they now have them on board for the rest of the race. Reasons for abandoning yacht were loose chain plate and a threat of the rig coming down. A bit odd as the unwritten rule of seamanship is to always step up to a life raft. Even stranger when two days later the same yacht is sighted still afloat with mast standing.

Most of the race we hand steer but it is so dark and difficult to make out the horizon we revert to the Raymarine automatic pilot. After only four hours of use it gives up the ghost and we discover the next day that it had blown a seal in the hydraulic, which is very disappointing.

Day 9. Light winds and a frustrating yachtsman's day. A decision is required today to motor or not. In the race rules you can motor and take a penalty. It could work for or against you so we are holding out in the hope that wind is not far away.

Day 10. Last night a squall came through and knocked us down in the dark. We didn't see it coming, but with all hands on deck we recovered. The edge of an eastern wave (a strong wind system off Africa) came through, one minute it was 12 knots and then in the space of a few minutes we were on our side in 35 knots. Complete calm followed with heavy rain. It's very frustrating, especially when it came in on the nose and we were sailing hard on the breeze for a short time.

An abandoned 12-metre open boat is reported 100 miles to the north of us. With no vision at night this is a scary thought. No wind, but we spot a sunfish sliding past the stern, then a phaeton Atlantic seabird flies overhead and that's our nature study for the day as we wait for wind. Every day so far we have managed to hold our position in the fleet's top 20, but slowly the bigger yachts behind are tracking us down.

Day 11. Slowly the wind filled in and we have the most stunning hot day. Trade winds from the east at 20 knots are cooling with a rolling 5-metre sea; the ocean is a gorgeous blue as is the sky with interesting trade wind clouds. We enjoy the sound system in the cockpit as everyone has their own iPod, with favourite Crowded House 'Weather with You' summing up our days. No one really misses the sweets I intentionally didn't buy (a decision that everyone agreed with at the time, but they still ask for them every day in the hope I might have some hidden away).

Day 12. The squall that went through last night was very scary. One minute we are sailing along doing 9 knots under a starry night and the next thing sneaking up behind us is a black cloud, under which you can see the rain looking like a mushroom. When it hits it's at 35 knots and the yacht instantly surges to 18 knots, driving rain drenches everyone and then it's all back to normal within 10 minutes.

Frustrated, Ian chases pressure systems to maximise boat speed; we have low pressure coming to the south and have gybed northwest to get better wind and angle for our home run. We are still maintaining 15th position before this move and will not know for another day whether skirting the light winds will pay off.

Day 13. Daylight arrives with an eastern wave wind system of 35 knots and we ease away on our final course to the northern end of St Lucia, 640 nautical miles to go or, as Ian puts it, 'one Sydney–Hobart Yacht Race'. Rain squalls all around us, we romp along riding the big rollers. The boys are in full wet weather gear which is not what you would expect on the 17th parallel and so close to the Caribbean.

Several squalls pass through at 30+ knots and after

The 2007 ARC gets under way

strapping down the spinnaker we manage to run with it. Landfall will be amazing. We can almost taste the rum punch, hear the beat of the drums and dance the salsa; anything different will be welcome.

As the race progresses the weight in the yacht gets lighter. In liquids alone we started with almost 1.4 tonnes made up of 500 litres of diesel, 500 litres of water, 120 x 1.5-litre water bottles, 240 cans of beer, 72 bottles of wine and 48 large bottles of soda water. And then there was the food!

Position results for 1200UTC Friday 7/12 have just been received and it appears as though we are still in a top position. The larger yachts start to roll through us but we are very favourably placed with the yachts that we had originally identified as the ones to beat.

iPod selection has now changed from 'Weather with You' to 'Ain't that a Kick in the Head' by Dean Martin.

Today is our 29th wedding anniversary, but becalmed – you could cut the air with a knife. Motoring and still racing, we can only assume every yacht around us is under the same conditions. The reason behind the cruising division being permitted to motor is that the organisers want you to get there within a reasonable time – and it *is* a very long way. Handicapping for motoring is based on a fast or slow race; no one knows that until the end.

Day 14. We go from trying to outrun rain squalls to chasing them in a matter of 24 hours. The eastern wave that goes through during the day causes a lot of damage to some of the other yachts and now has sucked all the air away from this area. Just our luck!

Day 15. Becalmed after a valiant night of going north to find wind, we start motoring. While inspecting the rig Ian notices the starboard lower stay is very slack and realises that something is wrong – he discovers the port lower spreader base has collapsed. Not wanting to put the rig in any danger of going over the side our race for handicap win is over. Securing the rig with inner forestay and lines to the affected area as best we can, we will now motor-sail the 280 miles to the finish line. We are still in the race and will now go for a good position over the line.

After working so hard it is soul-destroying to have to finish in this way, especially after all the effort put in by the crew. So much preparation went into ensuring that we were race-ready and our strategy was going to plan. It's been a very long and exhausting two weeks at sea and we never expected to do so well, only wanting a result we could be proud of. 'You can take the boys out of racing but you can't take racing out of the boys.' It is, after all, only a rally. *Cape Finisterre* has excelled herself and Ian is thrilled at the way she performs.

After a day listening to the rig making strange noises as we rolled over each wave, it is a long 230-nautical-mile journey motor-sailing to the finish. A further rig inspection during the day reveals that both the top spreaders have also torn away from the pins at the front of the mast end. More lines are attached to steady the mast and with careful handling we manage to sail through the finish line; a rule of the race.

Land ahoy! The finish line is a welcome sight at 2237 hours local time on 11 December. Finishing in 24th place over the line, we've spent 15 days 13 hours and 37 minutes at sea covering 2712 nautical miles. Now lined up with all the big boats, we are very happy with our result; we are the first of the five Australian yachts and the first Beneteau.

As it happens no one got sick and there were no injuries during the crossing. We enjoyed very good meals and everyone was in good spirits on arrival. Apart from a mast problem, which is another story, other crew sustained various broken bones and there were a lot of broken booms. Tragically, one owner died when hit by the boom during an involuntary gybe. As I noted earlier, it's not a race to be taken for granted and at the end of it all we are very happy with the preparations we made for it.

What a welcome we receive! Cups of rum punch, bottles of Bounty rum, beer and baskets of delicious tropical fruit. Even Kevin stops drinking his Bundaberg rum to enjoy the local mix (talk about taking coals to Newcastle!).

Would I do it again? It was a long time at sea, but I didn't get seasick and I never at any time wanted to turn back. There were fabulous days and scary nights, but I don't have a need to do it again.

As for Ian, he was in his element with all the downhill sailing. We had only been without a gennaker for six hours until the rig damage was discovered on the last day. Almost as good as sex, he reckons. This is Ian's fourth crossing of the Atlantic, the first time in 1970 was the same route on the 72-ft *Stormvogel*, a previous Sydney–Hobart line honours winner – and also the yacht featured in the movie *Dead Calm* starring Nicole Kidman and Sam Neill. The amazing thing is that trip took 14 days on a fast ocean racer – and on our cruising yacht we did it almost as quickly.

Ian's Cruising Notes
AUTOMATIC IDENTIFICATION SYSTEM (AIS)

This new system, the latest 'must have' on all cruising yachts, identifies ships and transmits their details including speed and course to your chart plotter via a VHF radio aerial. It's a great asset and we no longer have to rely on radar to track approaching ships. We only have a receiver on board at present but this season we are upgrading to the new Raymarine 500 AIS transponder and receiver that will allow ships to easily identify us as we approach their course.

The information received also includes the approaching ship's MMSI. If you have a new digital VHF radio you can call them up directly by keying in this identification number (a good idea as ships rarely stand by on channel 16 these days). You can apply for your MMSI when registering your yacht as a ship with your national authority and on receiving your digital radio operator's licence.

First Season
St Lucia–Antigua–Grenada

Life in the Caribbean

After our huge effort in the ARC, then getting our damaged rig back safely without losing it over the side, we have been working hard to try and resolve the issues. This is not made easy by the Christmas and New Year holidays now in full swing, but at least we find in Martinique excellent repair services. It's also an ideal place to motor around and enjoy the Caribbean way of life in its beautiful bays. Then there are the jazz evenings, all the swimming and the lovely people. Our stay in Rodney Bay, St Lucia, is very enjoyable catching up with all our fellow Australian competitors and friends from our time in Las Palmas. The ARC party side of the organisation again excels as along with various steel bands and plenty of rum punch we celebrate our crossing of the Atlantic.

This is the rainy month and it sure can rain. But it does pass and then out comes the sun again. What strikes us on arrival is the lush green landscape. As our crew slowly disperses, the remaining few rent a wagon and drive around St Lucia. We also climb Gros Piton, a conical 799-metre mountain that along with its conical neighbour represent the symbol of St Lucia. Most of them make the climb to the top, but Ian and I stop to enjoy the halfway view; it's magnificent.

The island is struggling economically since its independence and the only legacy the English left here was their bureaucratic system. Customs formalities in and out are archaic and very time-consuming. For some reason, if you are Australian, you have to get a US$50 visa each time you come in. Suddenly our New Zealand passports come in very handy. Mind you, maybe it's not entirely the fault of St Lucia. Australia is one of the few countries that insist on its visitors obtaining visas so looks like a bit of tit for tat.

Motoring north to Martinique is another blast from the past for Ian, especially when we anchor off Club Med at Les Boucaniers, Sainte Anne. He worked here for six months as a GO (Gentil Officer) back in 1972 teaching sailing – and a few other things, too, by the glazed look in his eyes. A few days later we visit the palm grove set on a beautiful beach where Club Med is located and after much negotiation we are given a guided tour. We meet a woman who's been working here for 35 years who remembers Ian (who back then had long hair and more on his mind than teaching young girls how to sail) as a 'very naughty boy'.

Entering Marin Harbour we are quickly reminded of the presence of coral reefs as either side of the channel markers we can see yachts washed up high and dry. Then, after we reach the marina, we experience a major shock when we learn that our mast has a serious kink and that it will be necessary to have a replacement mast fitted in Martinique – after it's been shipped out from France. Bugger!

Martinique is a French Department and, as such, it benefits from all the perks of mainland France. French goods are readily available and the currency is the euro.

After anchoring in Marin, we rent a car and tour the island visiting rum distilleries and the ruins of the once capital of Saint-Pierre, which was totally destroyed by the volcanic eruption of Mount Pelee in 1902 that killed 26,000 inhabitants bar one prisoner, who was saved by the protection offered by his stone cell. What comes as a surprise to us is that it wasn't lava, but hot gas and ash that destroyed the town.

Rum production in Martinique, much like wine in France, is controlled by the Appellation d'Origine Contrôlée (AOC), a French government standard that certifies the origin and production methods. The rum here is obtained by distilling the fermentation of fresh sugarcane juice. Other local (and definitely inferior) rums according to the proud rum manufacturers in Martinique are produced from what they call the sugar production leftovers, i.e. molasses. The French rum certainly has a distinctive flavour and when drunk in their signature mixture known as Ti Punch, it has an explosive effect on the taste buds.

Fish and lobster are plentiful on the island and from the roadside in Saint-Pierre we come across some local fishermen who are selling chunks of the huge tuna they have just caught. Using a machete, they chop off two large steaks for us.

We are on our own again as Nick and Michelle leave us, but our son Ian and his friend Nicola will join us early in the New Year. We celebrate Christmas Eve with John

Martinique is a French Department and, as such, it benefits from all the perks of mainland France. French goods are readily available and the currency is the euro.

Pitom Mountains, St Lucia (top)
Our daughter, Janey, enjoying a dip (bottom left)
and son, Ian, with a freshly caught dorado (bottom right)

Ian's Cruising Notes
INTERNET

Internet access improves every year and in most places we can use facilities ashore (at a café or club) for no charge or even on board if we are close to a resort. In the Lesser Antilles services are available for a small monthly subscription.

Our current wifi aerial, a High Power USB 2.0 Wireless Adapter with a USB extension cable with inbuilt booster, sits on the boom and has been known to receive from over 2 nautical miles away. However, it does take time to find a hotspot and sometimes we have to go ashore where for the price of a coffee in a resort we will be given their code.

and Sue Gilder from *Story Teller* and John and Irene Hunt from *Southern Princess*. We take all three yachts to the beautiful bay of Grande Anse where we have dinner at Ti Sable, a beachside restaurant. Lots of French families plus Santa Claus arrive by dinghy, showering all the children with fake snow and handing out wonderful presents; it certainly is a delightful night.

Ian and I stay on in this beautiful bay, but we aren't alone for long as we join up with more ARC Australians: Hans and Susanne Pettersson and daughters on their new Hanse 540. They call it their New York apartment and as we enjoy cocktails by candlelight on board, we have to agree they have their boat very well set up.

We are now alternating between Marin Harbour, the beach of Sainte Anne and Club Med. It's an enjoyable time with plenty of reading, swimming – and lots of the local rum as we wait for the Europeans to get back to work on 3 January so that we can keep things rolling with our replacement mast.

The Grenadines

For the last two weeks we have motored south (without our mast) from Martinique to the Grenadine Islands and back again with Ian and Nicola. It's time to forget our repairs and just enjoy the islands.

Looking a little odd without our mast we motor across the channel to St Lucia for a night in Marigot Bay including a wonderful dinner ashore in the rainforest. The sheltered bay, once frequented by pirates, is a 'Hurricane Hole' as well as being home to a gorgeous resort. Several movies including *Dr Dolittle* and *Pirates of the Caribbean* have been filmed here.

As the rainy season is still upon us we are like yoyos in the night opening and shutting hatches as the rain passes through, leaving us feeling hot and stuffy. We hear about a couple on a cruising yacht being attacked and robbed by three men in a bay on St Vincent Island so we invest in a hand-held flare pistol. Bypassing St Vincent, we experience a long day motoring 52 nautical miles to get to the island of Bequia where we can clear customs for the Grenadine Islands. It is a little tiresome clearing in and out of these islands, because each time it means we have to put up the appropriate flag and deal with yet another customs agent.

Port Elizabeth on Bequia Island is a delightful natural harbour. Ashore, Ian and Nicola come across a steel band and end up salsa dancing in the sand. Not far away Princess Margaret Beach (named after the British princess) with its turquoise-coloured waters and white sand beach lined with palm trees is a welcome and picturesque anchorage. Seven miles away is the peaceful billionaire's island of Mustique. Although privately owned, it can be still enjoyed by the public. Princess Margaret was the first to own a house here in 1968. Current owners include Mick Jagger, Tommy Hilfiger, Shania Twain and Bryan Adams, who were all present during our stay. We hire ourselves what is locally known as a mule, i.e. an open jeep, and go 'mansion hunting' around the island. On the way we have to watch out for land tortoises crossing the road; one has to stop and carry them out of the way. Our mansion hunt is successful and we even get to see through the secluded modern waterfront home on its private beach belonging to Bryan Adams, the well-known Canadian musician.

Indulging ourselves while we're here we frequent the famous Basil's Bar, the Cotton House Beach Café and Firefly Restaurant which are all very stylish and feature

The glamorous island of Mustique

Andrea on Tobago Cays

flying fish on the menu. During the ARC the lights on board the yacht would attract flying fish to land on the deck during the night so that when the sun rose the next day they'd start to smell really bad. But even that experience is not enough to put us off and we try them; they are absolutely delicious.

Only 20 nautical miles south are Tobago Cays, numerous uninhabited small islands that on our approach make the most impressive sight we've seen so far in this part of the world. Set in the crystal-clear electric-blue ocean, the islands have white sand beaches with coconut palms swaying in the breeze, protected by a crescent-shaped reef – it doesn't get any more perfect than this. With the protected anchorages here it's possible to stay the night along with many other boats; this place is no secret. As soon as we arrive we can't resist the temptation to go snorkelling and swim with the turtles.

For three days in water temperatures of 28°C young Ian and Nicola photograph coral out on the reef, swim with turtles only metres from the boat and observe a huge iguana basking in the sun on a rocky outcrop.

A range of T-shirts, along with fresh bread and crayfish, are sold by the cheerful locals with their gold-filled teeth, who come alongside in their colourful open long boats – one of their T-shirts says it all: 'Live slow – sail fast'.

Dragging ourselves away, we move on to yet another beautiful island, Mayreau and Saltwhistle Bay. There's nothing commercial about this island, which has only had electricity since 2003. The locals still catch their own water and own just seven cars between them. Coconut palms reach out over the sandy beach and the few inhabitants here sell colourful sarongs, shells and lobsters. It's a totally unspoilt island and we spend our days just absorbing our surrounds.

Ian's Cruising Notes
CUSTOMS AND IMMIGRATION

A set of ship's papers, which list country of registration, details of ownership etc, must be carried by all yachts, along with passports for each passenger. In some instances current insurance documents for the yacht may also be required. As a general rule islands of British heritage require the most paperwork and associated fees. The French islands are quite casual and you can enter the required data yourself on the customs' office computer. The islands of Spanish heritage are quite different and you can expect a personal visit from the authorities, while in Cuba at least five different authorities are likely to arrive every time you enter and depart a port. As your exit document (from the last island you visited) will always be required on entry to the next place, it pays to be diligent about keeping your paperwork up to date.

Making our way back to Martinique, we return to Bequia Harbour and there, in front of us, is a familiar-looking double-ended yacht *Freya*, from Sydney. Convinced that it can't possibly be the three-time winner of the Sydney–Hobart Yacht Race we discover that indeed it is the same yacht. We're lucky to catch the owner John Corbett on board and he makes us welcome. *Freya* was built by Lars Halvorsen and Sons and is still in her original state. John has owned her for 35 years and we have a somewhat ironic laugh over the fact that here we are with a five-month-old boat and no mast, yet *Freya* is 44 years old and still sailing. It is a great privilege to be on board this very famous yacht.

En route to St Lucia we catch a dorado fish as we punch into big seas, but we make good time. Anchoring beneath the two cone-shaped Piton Mountains, we enjoy sashimi, snorkel 'the wall' and the 'flower coral garden', drink cocktails in the resort ashore and watch the sun set. It's the first time we see the green flash. The sky on the horizon has to be very clear as it occurs just as the sun sets, you can't blink or you will miss seeing what some

Tobago Cays

Tobago Cays

call 'the passing-over green light'.

We have come to enjoy the west coast of St Lucia, the boat boys coming alongside with delicious tropical fruit for sale, the walking tours and the very friendly people. Daytime trips between the islands have been very pleasant and with plenty of wind from the NE it could have been – if we had a mast – wonderful sailing.

Le Grand Carnaval de la Martinique

Salines Beach on the southern end of Martinique offers the perfect crystal-clear seawaters that we come back to, again and again. Its arc of long white sand lined with palm trees – and the opportunity for some perving by the men – is hard to beat. On the beach, tartan hammocks swing between the palms and local women sell coconut ice-cream from a wooden churn. Friends of Ian's come

and go and we pass our days snorkelling, swimming and in the evening visiting Creole restaurants.

Fresh tropical and seasonal fruits are the highlight for Ian and his friend Caro, who left a few days ago. Everywhere are passionfruit, pawpaw and pineapples, plus avocados in which the flesh is thicker and the flavour more intense than we are used to. After a day of sunshine, guacamole is our latest craving along with fresh lime rum mojitos.

Congratulating ourselves on our perfect timing, we motor to Fort de France for the four days of pre-Lent carnival. We anchor beneath St Louis fort; there is no way Ian is going to miss this parade. Everyone dresses up, whether it's for the wicked street parties or just for the hell of cross-dressing or perhaps wearing a devil's outfit. It's a time for the whole family to have fun in their brightly coloured costumes. We notice that there are no

A bit of colour on Mayreau (top and bottom)

Scenes from Le Grand Carnaval de la Martinique (top and right)

barricades, no police and very little organisation, but everything is relaxed and a lot of fun.

Over each of the next four days there is a themed parade around a set circuit of the old town including along the waterfront.

Day one, Dimanche Gras, which starts at 3 pm, is Le Grand Carnaval de la Martinique. There are two parades just one street apart. One features floats from different districts showing the various cultural heritages on the island, from slavery to flower ladies, while in the next street it's full-on drag, so anything goes. Around the town they dance, following the bamboo and drum bands belting out the traditional hypnotic reggae tunes, with everyone joining in. The two parades come together with no inhibitions.

Day two, Lundi Gras, is Mariage Burlesque, a gender-bending mock wedding day in which the males are the brides and the females the grooms, followed by attendants, guests, priests and cakes to make up the party. We remain bewildered regarding the point of this parade but it is very funny.

Day three, Mardi Gras (Shrove Tuesday) Vide en Rouge is red day – sexy devil day. The town is awash in red and once again from 3 pm around and around the town everyone goes following 'The Pied Piper' while the drum bands beat out.

Day four, Mercredi des Cendres (Ash Wednesday), is Vide en Noir et Blanc (black and white for Lent) then the burning to ashes of Satan to mark the end of Carnaval. Around and around they go, hypnotised in their attempt to rid themselves of the devil for the rest of the year. Nothing much is different from the previous few days; maybe just the dress code.

The sound of drums beating in my ears lasts for days but

what do we think about Le Carnaval de la Martinique? It certainly isn't for the moral-minded and it lacks the sophistication of Rio, but what makes it fun is the happy time everyone has. The whole family dresses up so that you could well spot granddad in grandma's shoes, a boy living out his fantasy of being a terrorist, girls with braided coloured hair and various bewildered children watching dad dressed as a sexy woman – it all adds to the carnival atmosphere.

What really impresses us is the total integration of all the different cultures: from the original Caribs (Indians from South America), Africans via slavery, Indians post-slavery, French Europeans and people from what were French-ruled Asian colonies all intermarried and, from appearances, all living together very happily. It seems that the way the French administer their Caribbean territories includes providing the locals with all the social welfare benefits that are available in France, which results in economic benefits for the islands.

The only people missing are the Arawaks, the original South American Indian settlers who were eaten by the Caribs when the latter arrived in the twelfth century. It's said that the Caribs would castrate and then fatten young boys to eat and utlise the women to breed out the Arawak genes. Mind you, the Catholic Europeans didn't behave much better when they arrived in the 1600s when they drastically depleted the numbers of Caribs.

Pointe du Bout, Martinique

With our wings still clipped (i.e. no mast), we stay in one bay for two weeks, living aboard and idly passing time. A small peninsula just across the bay from Fort-de-France, Pointe du Bout is Martinique's 'shore area', with several small manmade beaches and some of the island's largest resorts. As we sit and wait we read, get to know the locals, as well as some of the visiting Europeans staying in the resorts, and plan our next three years.

It's good for us to slow down, especially me, because I am not immune to getting sick. Fortunately, the SOS medical service for yachts offers a very good service here in Martinique and the second time we have cause to call the doctor he is waiting at the dock 10 minutes later. It is nothing too serious; just a virus that takes time to get over.

Getting Ian to sit on the resort beach area, relax and do nothing has never been easier given the number of topless women and models parading beach wear. Many mojitos are enjoyed during this enforced break during which we meet Geordie and Patricia Burnett-Stuart who are here on holiday from Europe and who join us on our cruise at a later stage.

Within walking distance is the Pagerie Estate and Museum, an eighteenth-century sugar plantation and birthplace of the Empress Josephine, whom Napoleon Bonaparte married in 1796.

Wandering through the charming stone cottage, garden

and ruins of a sugar mill set in the lush green tranquil countryside fills in another day. All over the island there are reminders of the Empress of France. Josephine already had two children by a previous marriage when she married Napoleon and although they had no children together, her daughter married Napoleon's brother. Their son, Louis, grew up to take the French throne as Napoleon III in 1852.

Slavery, abolished in 1848, is another part of the local history. We visit the museum in Fort-de-France and the Savane des Esclaves, a typical village of the kind inhabited by slaves back then, but still very little is said about the injustice. It all started when early settlers planted sugarcane plantations in the seventeenth century and needed labour. Several million people were kidnapped from their homelands to become victims of the slave trade in the New World plantations. At one time slaves outnumbered the colonials in Martinique, but thanks to the abolition this remains a milestone in their history.

It's of interest to us that the practice of slavery was

Anse Mitan looking across to Fort-de-France, Martinique

Market, Fort-de-France   *Birthplace of Empress Josephine, Anse Mitan*

abolished in 1794 while Martinique was under English rule. Then, in 1802, Martinique was restored to the French and Napoleon and Josephine reintroduced the practice.

A strike in the port of Fort-de-France has just been announced. The ship with our new mast has arrived – we can actually see it across the bay, but the locals are saying it's going to be a long strike. We're not happy campers!

Up and sailing in Martinique

For 26 days we haven't lifted the anchor and we've been making all our own water and power – a good test of our self-sufficiency. Due to the very warm sea, barnacles cover our anchor and our hull looks like the Garden of Eden, but with the help of local divers we are soon shipshape again.

Holed up beside us is *Intrepid* from New Zealand and we enjoy many nights with its owners, either on their boat or on ours, eating delicious roast leg of lamb imported from New Zealand, listening to music from the sixties and drinking a wine or two. The bays are full of yachts but not many from Down Under, which is disappointing.

Putting a show on for us, sailing in and around the anchored cruising yachts are the traditional local fishing craft called *yoles*. They're now used for racing, a local version of 18-footers, but nothing fancy – not even a harness; these guys hang out on poles.

By the time we are sailing again I should have my head around the 'Red, Right Returning' for entering a harbour. (When entering a Commonwealth or European port, the red buoy is always on the port side. But in the Caribbean they use the American system with the red

Ian's Sailing Notes
ANCHORING

In the Caribbean it is always easy to find a sheltered anchorage. In fact, over the two seasons we were there, we anchored out at least 95 per cent of the time but with only two of us on board (except for visiting family and friends), it had to be a simple and easy procedure. Our primary anchor is a 65 lb CQR (plough) with 75 metres of 12 mm chain and an additional 45 metres of heavy warp; we can lower it without leaving the wheel using an electric windlass control and counter. We normally let out seven times our depth, then just let the yacht drift back and naturally set itself in sand over about 20 minutes, rather than force the anchor to set. If the anchorage is crowded we reduce it to five times our depth and in shallow water we let out to 10 times. Once settled, I attach a 4-metre snubber line to the chain and back to a deck cleat to take the spring and stop the chain crunching.

For a back-up or stern anchor we use a lightweight alloy Fortress FX-37 anchor (9.5 kg) that is equivalent to a 55-lb standard anchor and which grips really well. Using just a heavy braided warp it is easy for me to pull it up by hand and when used off the stern, it can keep us heading into the waves on windless nights.

For emergencies we also carry a spare 55-lb Delta anchor with 25 metres of 12-mm chain and 50 metres of heavy braided warp.

buoy on the starboard side.) The 'Red, Right Returning' rhyme helps people to remember to keep the red buoy on the starboard side as they enter port or they will end up on a reef.

Three months after damaging the mast, almost exactly to the day, our sails are up and it's, 'Oh, what a feeling!' as the motor is silenced and we begin our first sail in the Caribbean. There is no horizon; the turquoise sky meets the turquoise sea and with the wind always from the northeast our sea trial is exhilarating. Ian is in his element, tacking, hard on into the wind; every angle is sailed to test the rig. He's got one eye on the mast and the other on the depth, which can be deceptive because the sea is so crystal clear. It's a very eerie feeling being able to see the bottom.

Dominica

With our new mast installed we plan to sail north to Antigua and take part in the forty-first Antigua Sailing Week at the end of April. We also have to make plans for storing the yacht at the end of the season as the hurricane season is approaching.

Leaving the Windward Islands for the Leeward Islands we are never out of sight of the next island. Perfect conditions, winds of 21 knots on the beam; tide going west, it couldn't get any better. Between most of the islands is only about 20–25 miles of open sea, otherwise we are in the shelter of the land. Loving being able to sail again, we head out of south Martinique to Prince Rupert Bay in Dominica, 68 nautical miles north. It is our first long sail in the Caribbean where the wind strength and direction are constant, meaning perfect reaching up and down the islands.

Dominica, the most undeveloped island in the Caribbean, doesn't disappoint us on approach, with rugged green forest covering the volcanic mountains. Independent since 1978, with a population of only 70,000, the island has not been taken over by tourism. We are greeted by an assortment of boat boys, each one trying to be first to claim us. 'I'll look after you for your stay, take you on tours, collect your rubbish' and so on. All at a charge, of course. We choose Providence to be our 'mon' and he takes us on the Indian River cruise. Bloodwood trees line the river with their amazing root formation, and we enjoy the sight of hummingbirds, parrots and lizards all living in this ecological-friendly environment. Dominica is promoting itself as an eco island and in doing so has gained financial support from the EU. The shores are rubbish-free and all fishing and diving activity must be done under licence. In fact, cruising yachts aren't even allowed to troll along the coast.

Dominica is an English island lying between two French Islands, Martinique to the south and Guadeloupe to the north. As such it was in a very strategic position during the

Napoleonic Wars in the nineteenth century and many forts were built here. Fort Shirley in Prince Rupert Bay is being magnificently restored (with EU money) with 17 of the original 34 cannons still in place. The fort saw no action as it was enough for it to look very intimidating, but the major naval battle between the English and French took place in the channel to the north.

The locals are very friendly, especially the children. They want to touch my hair and even ask for a ride in our inflatable dinghy. It is nice to have a language in common and we feel we are in a very special place of natural wonders.

While we are enjoying breakfast one morning, we are lucky to sight two whales at the entrance of the bay. This is the season they come down to the Caribbean from the Arctic, making them annual visitors to this idyllic place.

We drive through lush banana plantations, plus orchards of orange and grapefruit trees, to reach a rainforest at the foot of Morne Diablotins, Dominica's highest mountain. By 11 o'clock we are walking a trail that takes us through 100-metre-tall century-old trees that totally dwarf us. It's raining, naturally, but the fresh cool air is welcome and we lift our heads toward the daylight high above, filtering through a canopy of leaves. This magnificent forest has only survived because it was too difficult to mill commercially. The island boasts a total of 365 rivers so there are plenty of waterfalls; while in the rainforest we visit the most spectacular of these, the Syndicate waterfall.

Only the locals know the secret road that takes you to a special deserted beach on the northwest coast. It features black sand, white foam, breaking sea – all overhung by tall coconut palms.

At 5 o'clock (it doesn't pay to be late) we settle in to watch the sun set over the rainforest at Indigo Restaurant where the birds fly in and out from the lush tropical forest below. Perched high up in a tree Swiss Family Robinson-style, the restaurant furniture is made from driftwood and features just one table so one has to book well in advance. Maria, the owner and chef, came to this island as a visitor from France many years ago, married a local and never went home. Her menu

The group of islands comprising Iles des Saintes belongs to Guadeloupe. We pass a number of stunning turquoise-coloured bays, then anchor beneath a pretty village set in a barren landscape.

The barren hills of Iles des Saintes (top)
Banana twit (bottom left)
Looking through Fort Josephine ruins to Bourg des Saintes (bottom right)

includes produce from her garden or whatever can be harvested from the trees in and around the forest. We start with a fresh grapefruit rum punch and end with coconut cream ice-cream with ginger. What more could you ask for on a balmy humid evening? The latest of the *Pirates of the Caribbean* movies was filmed here on Dominica and its star, Johnny Depp, was a frequent guest of Maria's.

People on the yachts around us are warning of a storm up north that has produced a 5-metre swell and which will roll through the Caribbean for three days. Not pleasant conditions for sailing between islands, so we will have to stay put in this magnificent bay for a little longer.

Iles des Saintes

The wind is calling and the swell has disappeared so Ian wants to move on. Up at 6 am, we see the sunrise as we sail in a flat sea to Iles des Saintes (Islands of the Saints) only 18 miles north; all in a day's work. At 8 am we hook a 35-kg sailfish (it looks like a marlin), which puts up quite a fight for about 30 minutes before we land it. Soon there's blood everywhere, but we now have 25 beautiful steaks in the freezer. Ian did an amazing job of getting the fish on board; when I see the rod bend literally into a circle, all I want to do is cut it free.

The group of islands comprising Iles des Saintes belongs to Guadeloupe. We pass a number of stunning turquoise-coloured bays, then anchor beneath a pretty village set in a barren landscape. We can't believe the difference between Dominica and this amazingly dry place. Obviously the Caribbean has not been exempt from the strange weather that the rest of the world has been experiencing.

This time of year is meant to be the dry winter season, but in the week we are here we experience high winds and rain squalls most days. We actually haven't minded too much because it is still hot and the odd shower cools us down, but the long-time cruisers and locals say they have never known a season like this one.

We are now sailing in unison with Heinz and Elizabeth (Liz) Oser, long-time friends who live in France but who are here on a chartered yacht out of Pointe-a-Pitre,

Ian's Cruising Notes
PHOTOGRAPHY

Cameras and water do not go well together and we've had to replace several damaged by water. Even though we always use a watertight bag for taking our camera ashore accidents happen, sometimes when one of us is trying to get that special shot.

We travel with two cameras: a versatile digital single lens reflex 12 mega-pixel model with a lens that operates from wide to zoom at 18-200 and which is great for getting close to the action. Our back-up camera is a small pocket-sized 10 mega-pixel model that can also operate underwater.

Every evening we download that day's images (sometimes up to 200) onto the computer, sorting and deleting as we go. It's an especially enjoyable exercise because we get to relive some of the really great experiences.

Guadeloupe, which offers a very sheltered harbour and a marina with a fantastic yacht base for provisioning. There are also plenty of islands within easy reach for day sailing. Guadeloupe, though, is an interesting butterfly-shaped island; one 'wing' is flat while the other is mountainous. Our first impression is of the beautiful colour of the sea; there are miles and miles of shallow sky-blue coastline along the southeast wing. Ilet du Gosier, only three miles away, is where we anchor for a night. Here we swim and later, lying comfortably in bed, listen to the waves breaking on the reef.

Visiting the town of St Francois on Guadeloupe is an interesting exercise because of the very narrow entrance through the coral reef to the lagoon. With a strong easterly blowing, we motor 20 nautical miles into the big rolling seas hoping as we go that the large waves will not be breaking at the entrance. But once inside the reef, we find the lagoon is very safe and proves to be a comfortable anchorage. Locals Philippe and Marianne, friends of the Osers, entertain us ashore at the new marina, which is full of shops and several very good restaurants.

Ian's Cruising Notes
FISHING

I finally caught the fishing bug and bought myself a good rod, which I mounted on the transom. Now we simply let out a lure and line whenever we are at sea. The right lure is important, though, and we recommend Williamson Lures. For the Atlantic Coast we found green/red were best, red/pink over reefs in the eastern Caribbean and blue/purple or black/blue in the deep western Caribbean.

We always set up cleaning and cutting gear before we set sail, including a large chopping board, meat cleaver, mallet and a long filleting knife, and our large anchor wash pump has a hose connected back to the cockpit. As our fishing brings mostly very successful results (mostly dorado, sailfish, wahoo, Spanish mackerel and loads of tuna) the freezer is put to good use.

Tip 1: when attempting to land a large fish, we sometimes pour alcohol down the gill to stun it, making it easier to get it on board.

Tip 2: beware of *ciguatera*, a toxin found in large reef fish such as barracuda, red snapper, grouper and others. Caribbean guidebooks warn against eating them if they are caught in waters north of Guadeloupe or measure more than 1 metre in length.

Leaving the lagoon, which involves negotiating our way back through the heavy waves crashing at the entrance, we have a great sail to Marie-Galante. Twenty miles to the south, this island, constitutionally part of France as is Guadeloupe of course, is covered in sugarcane, producing the bulk of the local 59 per cent-proof rum.

What starts out as a great day though, doesn't end the same way – we're now anchored in Anse Carnot, a highly photogenic beach on Marie-Galante, and I can't resist swimming to shore. But I want to take some photographs once I get there so Ian offers to take my camera with him in the inflatable. The trouble starts when the sight of a woman in a red bikini frolicking in the sea proves to be too much of a distraction for him and the breaking surf picks up the inflatable, sending it sideways and tipping Ian into the water. Trying to hold the camera out of the water, he tears his hamstring and everything turns to custard. By the time I get to him he is in agony as well as feeling guilty (although the red bikini couldn't have cared less).

Walking is the best therapy and so we take the dinghy to the beach next to where we are anchored so Ian can get his exercise. Anse de Mayes is the most beautiful long beach we have seen so far this year. Without a camera, I'm unable to capture the colour, but it will remain in my memory forever. No doubt the red bikini – and its consequences – will also be an indelible memory for Ian.

With the wind behind us we enjoy a fast sail west back to Iles des Saintes. After entering between Fort Napoleon and the ruins of Fort Josephine, we anchor in the protected main harbour, which will end up being home for longer than we expect. With its cute seaside village, museum, crystal-clear waters and fabulous snorkelling, there's plenty to do so we're happy to shelter here until the winds and big seas subside.

Fort Napoleon has been well restored and is now a naval museum high on the hill above the main town of Bourg des Saintes. It is interesting to see the French side of the naval battle lost to the English in the straits to the south. Apparently the English had a lucky break when the wind changed and they managed to divide the French fleet. One thing we found quite disturbing were the models and drawings of the slave ships used to bring the Africans to the sugar plantations.

In the lee of Ilet a Cabrit, a small island not far from the main island of Les Saintes, we are able to put a stern line ashore and spend several wonderful days swimming in the beautiful clear water observing the colourful coral fish and the dive-bombing skills of the pelicans as they swoop down from a great height.

In time Ian's bruises disappear, and wind conditions improve. We both feel well and happy and manage to fill in our days doing nothing much at all.

Visiting the town of St Francois on Guadeloupe is an interesting exercise because of the very narrow entrance through the coral reef to the lagoon.

Bay on the west coast of Guadeloupe

English Harbour, Antigua

While we shelter under Ilet a Cabrit waiting for the big seas and winds to abate, Liz and Heinz sail back to Pointe a Pitre in atrocious conditions. They have to return the yacht to the charter base before flying back to France.

Our sail from Iles des Saintes to the coastal western wing of Guadeloupe is fast and lumpy, but as soon as we are behind the mountains it's flat calm and no wind. Halfway up the coast is Pigeon Island and the recently renamed Jacques Cousteau Underwater Park (Cousteau considered this to be one of the finest dive sites in the world). Perfect diving in 12 metres; this park with its deep but clear blue water showcases nature at its best. We snorkel over interesting rock formations, coloured fish, octopus and moray eels, the sight of which send me, flippers flapping, very quickly back to the boat.

A year ago a statue to Jacques Cousteau was mounted here under the water and after persisting for a while we eventually find it. Set on a white sand patch, facing a coral-encrusted cliff teeming with fish, it is in very deep water.

Deshaies Harbour on the northwestern tip of Basse Terre is home for a few days while we explore the rainforest-clad mountains of Basse Terre. High above the pretty fishing village of Deshaies is Le Jardin Botanique (Botanic Garden) and after a bit of exercise getting up to it we discover it to be one of the best-maintained gardens we have seen to date. Tropical flowers and plants are everywhere; lots of pink pelicans and native birds, too. I can only dream about the new camera I will have before too long, but in the meantime Ian's waterproof 'sardine can' will suffice.

We love Guadeloupe's diversity – from the flat dry land, white sand and shallow turquoise seas on one side

English Harbour, Antigua

to the towering lush green rainforests and deep seas on the other.

Making the 42-mile crossing to Antigua couldn't be better and it only takes us five hours in the northeasterly trade winds. We base ourselves in the protected English Harbour and admire the superyachts all around us, happy to settle in here for a few weeks, especially as English is widely spoken and Antigua Sailing Week, which has been an annual event for 41 years attracting over 180 entries from around the world, is about to start. The large cruising division has five races, all of which we have entered, and we are looking forward to the many parties over the next few days. The first major event is the 21st Antigua Classic Yacht Regatta, which starts on 17 April, followed 10 days later by the racing and cruising division regatta that we have entered.

The Classic regatta will be a new experience for us

and some famous craft from a bygone era are gathering ready to participate. Ian is drooling over yachts such as *Ticonderoga*, the maxi to beat in her day, still looking immaculate; the 136-ft J Class *Ranger*, and the wonderful gaff-rigged schooners *Eleonora*, a Herreshoff 120-footer, and *Altair*, a Fife 108-footer. Over 50 classic boats, ranging from 30 ft to 148 ft will be racing.

Of special interest to us is the arrival of the old round-the-world racing ketches from New Zealand: *Steinlager* and *Fisher & Paykel*, which have come for our sailing week. And of particular interest to Ian is *Charisma*, a 55-footer that was a member of the 1973 USA Admirals Cup team when he was crewing on *Salty Goose*.

English Harbour is an amazingly sheltered anchorage. It was the home of the English fleet in the late eighteenth century and although Nelson's Dockyard was abandoned and subsequently closed in 1889, it has since

sea and shore, Antigua (top)
Lunch on the boat (bottom left)
Caribbean steel band (bottom right)

Ian's Cruising Notes
WEATHER

It's relatively easy for us to access various weather related websites such as www.buoyweather.com to which we subscribe and set up charts for particular cruising areas, and www.windguru.com, which provides an overall picture but because it is geared more towards surfing and kite boarding, it always reports on the weather side of an island.

When we can't access the Internet through a local site we use the iridium satellite phone. Our provider (mailasail) has a free system for supplying an up-to-date and reliable GRIB weather file for a requested area. The information is received within 30 minutes along with a chart of the location showing a 500-nautical mile radius for the hourly periods requested and featuring arrows depicting wind direction and strength.

The weather in the Caribbean is generally very predictable. Easterly trade winds blow during the cruising season (December to May), and they vary between blowing from the northeast through to the southeast from 15 to 25 knots every day, making for delightful easy sailing with the wind on the side of the yacht. Further into the northern Caribbean this system can be affected by the winter northers blowing down from the USA, which just means finding shelter for a couple of days.

been wonderfully restored. Nelson himself served here when at the age of 25 he was in command of a frigate with a complement of 250. Altogether, 5000 military personnel were based here during the Napoleonic wars but like all the other forts in the vicinity Fort Berkeley, now in ruins, never saw action.

You may remember one of my diary entries during the ARC last December relating to an abandoned yacht. *Barbary Duck*, the name of the abandoned boat, was left to float off the Cape Verde islands, but three months and 2000 nautical miles later it turned up here off the coast of Antigua – and today Ian and I saw her in a

boatyard. She actually looks very seaworthy and it is quite unbelievable that this Westerly Corsair 38 was ever abandoned in the first place. Her mast had broken at the lower spreader but she was not dismasted when found; despite the cracking around the chain plates that led the owners to believe the mast was in danger at the time. Abandoning her like that created a dangerous hazard for other yachts crossing the Atlantic and it makes us wonder what the people on board must have been thinking of to leave her when she was still floating and with her rig intact.

Sunday night is 'Jump Up' at Shirley Heights, overlooking English and Falmouth Harbour. As the sun goes down, and the steel band and reggae music break out, it's one big BBQ party. Using 44-gallon drums among other things, the enthusiastic band beats out everything from the Beatles' 'Let It Be' to a Mozart concerto. Absolutely amazing! Unfortunately we missed the previous Sunday when famous West Indian cricketers Curtly Ambrose and Richie Richardson performed with their band Dread and the Bald One. The whole island is cricket-mad with Sir Viv Richards, a former captain, the local hero and Ian loves telling the locals, 'Hi, I'm from Australia, the home of cricket!'

Getting the 'jump on' bus on several different occasions provides us with another musical experience. One day we rock along to loud reggae music and a Rastafarian driver steering to the music and the next day we sing along to a gospel service. We really love the good-natured locals – and while the West Indies is winning the cricket everyone is happy.

The island itself is quite small and the population (72,000) is not large either, but although it's a slightly scruffy place, the locals are the nicest and happiest we have come across; especially the children. Maybe it's the rum in the milkshakes.

Antigua

What a wonderful treat to be in Antigua for the Classic Yacht Regatta 2008. There will be more than 60 vessels competing from 148 ft down to 30 ft; our favourites are the vintage gaff-rigged yachts built between 1890 and 1915. There are some much more modern ones,

Whitehawk in a blur of action, Antigua Classic Race Week

some built just five years ago, but in each case they've been built to the original drawings, construction and rig. A vintage yacht appears to be the new toy of the month for those that have everything.

Between the two regattas and with Annie and Baney Richardson on board we take the opportunity to sail around to Green Island for a few days. On our approach to the entrance of the lagoon we spot a catamaran up on the reef – another reminder to be very careful of the local conditions. In this case the unfortunate owner was late leaving port and arrived in the dark to try to negotiate a narrow channel between reefs. There is no hope of salvage so the owner is trying to save everything possible.

We're amazed at the stunning shades of blue and green, the white sand and the conch shells everywhere. Conch is a local food and the beautiful shells lie broken all over the beach, but live ones can be spotted in very shallow water. It's very hard for us to accept the waste of these beautiful shells, but to the locals they treat them much as Kiwis and Australians do oysters.

Antigua Race Week 2008

'Cruising' is an interesting word, but it seems to mean different things to different people. Our line-up for the first race has Ian ('I'll show them!') in the front row and it's nearly over before it starts. We've entered the cruising division, which Ian assumes will be a casual start, but not so. The crew on the boat alongside quote the rules at us as we reach the top mark in second place and then several serious and fully crewed racing yachts attempt to mow us down. We soon come to realise this isn't cruising as we know it.

It's time to get serious so Ian whips us all into shape.

Baney and Annie Richardson from Sydney and Don Reid from Noosa have never sailed on our yacht before and by the end of the 23-mile race around the west coast to Fort James we are all exhausted – but very excited about our fifth place out of 16 in our division. We only missed third place by three seconds on our handicap so Ian tells us we will just have to try harder the next day.

The 41st Stanford Antigua Race Week attracts 185 yachts from around the world; 80 in Division A and 105 in Division B. The serious racing yachts are in Division A, including the 98-ft *Leopard* and the 90-ft *Rambler* (previously known as *Shockwave*), fighting it out with the TP 52s and other hot racing yachts. This division has seven races to complete.

Division B is broken down to 10 divisions, five for chartered bare boats. There are five races, each about 23 nautical miles long, to various bays on the island. All competing yachts have to be rated with the Caribbean rating certificate with several choices for rig: main and genoa, main and poled-out genoa, main and two genoas, and main genoa and spinnaker. We elect to race with poled-out genoa as we will be short-handed for some of the regatta.

Fort James Bay is a mass of yachts and one big beach party ashore with lots and lots of crayfish cooking on the barbecues; I think everyone on the island is here to join in. A live reggae band keeps us awake all night and we start to wonder if we are too old for this stuff.

Now it's time for race two and Ian puts more effort into the start. We have Phil and Ann Smith from New York joining us for two races so we are now a 'professional' crew of seven or pretend to be. Practically nudging the jade-coloured coral reefs and with Ian taking every advantage of the shifting breeze, we come

second and head back to English Harbour to celebrate.

The third race is a coastal sail along the southern side of the island. We want to go to the left side on the first beat to the top mark so Ian decides to be in the second row at the start line. But he spies a hole and can't resist taking it and once again we are in the thick of it leading around the mark. We finish fourth, but it's a been long hot day with the wind dropping below 5 knots, something we have not experienced in our five months in the Caribbean.

A welcome lay day is next and it's time to head for a bay for a quiet barbecue lunch and a swim. The island of Antigua boasts 365 bays, one for each day of the year.

The fourth race is to Jolly Harbour Marina for the night and it's down to Annie, Baney, Ian and me because Phil and Ann have gone back home and Don has departed with his yacht *Honeymoon*. Once he's back in the USA he'll haul her out for the hurricane season before he returns to Noosa.

For this fourth race Ian promises to take it easy as we are seriously under-crewed. No such luck, though, as a snide remark from one fully crewed yacht accuses us of reducing crew for the light conditions. The light wind is frustrating but after six hours of sailing and with a little bit of luck and cunning we manage to get another second.

After each race the top three yachts are presented with either a gold, silver or bronze pennant to fly from the backstay, a nice way to recognise results. Thanks to sponsor La Perla, the Jolly Harbour resort puts on the most enjoyable party at the local golf club with great food, rum and music.

Race five, the last race, involves sailing back to English Harbour. Although it's under blue skies, it's a challenging as well as exhausting sail with winds from zero to 20 knots, but we manage another fourth. Thank goodness there are only five races. This is the first time in nine months aboard that we have actually had to sail *Cape Finisterre* into the wind and tack. We are thrilled at the way she easily handles the conditions, especially against fully crewed yachts with lots of experience aboard.

Crew, champagne and sailing during Antigua Race Week (top left, top right and right)

Our fourth overall position in Antigua Sailing Week is a thrill and well worth all the effort. Except that due to being dehydrated after the last race I pass out and an ambulance has to be called. Ian vividly remembers the experience: me completely out to it, sirens blaring and then the ambulance suddenly coming to a halt because the oxygen has run out. The driver gets out and organises another bottle and we're on our way again until, nearing the hospital, the driver asks Ian if he would like a hamburger before they arrive because there won't be any food available. This is third world medical attention. The first thing I'm aware of when I regain consciousness is Ian whispering in my ear to 'get my act together; because I'm not going to like where I am'. Fortunately I don't experience any long-term effects and the incident acts as a reminder to stay safe and drink plenty of water.

As we pass the mid-winter mark we become aware that the weather is warming up and the sea temperature will rise to 28°C, all of which means the hurricane season is fast approaching. Most owners will start getting their boats ready for storage outside the hurricane belt (south of 12 degrees) around the end of May. Our plan is to sail 350 nautical miles south to Grenada where we will store the boat, taking three weeks to get there. Storage will mean hauling *Cape Finisterre* out of the water, placing her in a one-piece cradle and strapping her down to very deep anchor points in the compacted ground. We will strip the mast and deck of all the sails and halyards, remove the dodger and bimini and lay the boom on the deck. All this will reduce windage (i.e. reducing the service area that is exposed to the wind) should a hurricane pass through. We will keep our fingers crossed that it doesn't happen! But meanwhile Geoff and Pip Lavis

Luxurious Mustique (top)
Racing yoles, Marin, Martinique (bottom left)
Collecting sea urchins, Saltwhistle Bay (bottom right)

from Sydney join us for the sail to Grenada, and we have plenty of time to enjoy ourselves as we make our way back down the arc of 14 islands.

The end of another sailing season

The sail from Antigua to the eastern end of Guadeloupe is a bit close to the wind so we ease away and sail the 45 nautical miles to the northern end of the river that separates the two islands of Guadeloupe. Negotiating the channel between the buoys in the reef, and then meandering up the river through amazing mangroves we anchor for the night under the first bridge. Once a day at 0430 hours the bridge opens so it's an early start in the dark to negotiate the rest of the river and arrive at the second bridge, which opens at 0500 hours.

Whales, dorado and turtles, turquoise-coloured bays and glorious weather, our sail south with Pip and Geoff on board is adding up to the perfect Caribbean experience. We bay-hop, we swim, and we eat and we drink our way past island after island, most of which are looking very familiar as of course we have been here before. Pip can't believe the comfort of sailing in the Caribbean with warm weather, a 26°C sea and a constant breeze from the east. Then we experience a haze for the next few days, which turns out to be sand that's blown over from the Sahara desert. It's certainly spent a long time in the atmosphere as it crossed the Atlantic and it must make for poor visibility at sea.

Phil and Robbie on *Anteater Blues* meet up with us in Prince Rupert Bay, Dominica, for a fun evening; they are en route to deliver their yacht to Fort Lauderdale and then ship her to Brisbane.

A special treat for us in Marin, Martinique, is watching the start of the Yole Regatta; the boats have come from all around the island to compete in the regatta. Fitted with bamboo masts and wooden poles, they are capable of going fishing out at sea for up to five days. These days they are used for racing, usually with a crew of 20, with a beach start and once in the water not a harness in sight. One could compare them to the 18-footers that sail on Sydney Harbour.

Between St Lucia and St Vincent a huge dorado takes our rolling lure and before we get it on board we spot two whales cruising beside us. In rolling conditions and doing 9 knots it's an urgent call to luff up and roll up the headsail as Ian struggles to land it because we are not sure of the whales' intentions. Fortunately they move on and we are soon enjoying barbecued fresh fish with fresh pineapple on curried rice for lunch before we even get to the next island.

Our next stop is for a swim at Princess Margaret Beach on Bequia, followed by cocktails at sunset on Mustique and then a snorkel with the turtles at beautiful blue Tobago Cays. In between we are on port tack sailing rather than motoring between the islands.

Saltwhistle Bay on Mayreau Island is voted Number One by everyone on board for its crystal-clear water, perfect anchorage and half-moon bay of golden sand lined with coconut palms. What more could one ask for? The local boys are cleaning sea urchins off Palm Island and advise our menfolk that if they'd like to spend the night 'cabin jabbin' they should mix the pulp of the urchins with some white wine.

Then it's time to check out of the Grenadines and sail to the island of Carriacou where we feast on the local mangrove oysters, fresh from the swamp, washed down with a bottle or two of French white wine.

We arrive in Prickly Bay, Grenada, where we spend two days preparing the yacht for hauling for the hurricane season. This involves placing it in a one-piece cradle, which is then firmly tied to strong anchor points made of steel rods set deep in concrete. Should a hurricane blow through, there's now no way the yacht can fall over and cause any damage to itself or other craft nearby.

It's been a long but exciting 10 months on our new yacht; and am looking forward to getting the sand out of my shoes. Sailing from the 42nd north parallel south to the 12th, i.e. from France to the tropical Caribbean, covering in excess of 6000 nautical miles has been a challenging but hugely rewarding experience – especially the Atlantic crossing.

Cocktails

Cuban Mojito

A long and refreshing drink.

1 handful mint leaves
4 Tbsp sugar
juice of 5 limes
4 limes, sliced
1 cup white Havana Club Rum
2 cups soda water
ice

Place first 4 ingredients in a 2-litre jug and gently pound together with a wooden mortar and pestle to infuse. Add rum and soda water and top with ice.

Note: To make a Mojito Royal, substitute champagne for the soda water.

Pina Colada

1 cup white rum
3 cups ripe pineapple pieces
2 tbsp cane sugar
½ cup coconut cream
crushed ice

Blend all ingredients together.

For a special look, dress glass with a wedge of fresh pineapple, cherries and a colourful straw.

Ti Punch

Per glass:
5 measures rum
1 Tbsp cane sugar
juice of 1 lime
ice cubes

Combine all ingredients.

Dominican Rum Special

1 cup white rum
2 Tbsp honey
juice of 4 pink grapefruit
pink grapefruit pulp or extra juice
ice
pink grapefruit wedges for garnish

Combine rum and honey in a 2-litre jug (it's very important to completely dissolve the honey in the rum). Add grapefruit juice and use some of the pulp or make up to 3 cups with extra grapefruit juice.

Top with ice and serve with a wedge of pink grapefruit.

Daiquiri

juice of 6 limes
⅓ cup sugarcane juice
1 cup rum
1 cup soda water
dash of bitters (optional)
ice

Combine lime juice, sugar, rum and soda water in a jug. Add bitters if wished. Top with ice.

Espresso Martini

1 part Crème de Cacao
1 part Tia Maria
1 part vodka
1 part espresso coffee

Put all ingredients in a cocktail shaker filled with ice. Shake well and strain into a large martini cocktail glass.

Daiquiri (left) and Pina Colada
Conch Shack, Virgin Islands

Cayman Rum and Coke

Per glass:
1 measure rum
1 measure coke
juice of 1 lime
ice

Combine all ingredients. The lime cuts the sweetness in the coke.

Flamed Bananas

1 ripe banana per person, peeled and
    cut in half lengthwise
oil for frying
cane sugar
rum
lime juice
whipped cream for serving

Place bananas in an oiled frying pan, sprinkle with cane sugar and cook lightly. Pour in rum, heat and light with match.
    Serve with a squirt of lime juice and some whipped cream.

Pineapple Gazpacho

pineapple
cane sugar
whipped cream or coconut ice-cream for serving
rum (optional)

Very finely slice pineapple and spread on heatproof platter. Sprinkle with cane sugar and grill under hot grill until the sugar caramelises. Pour on rum if using, heat and light with match.
    Serve with whipped cream or coconut ice-cream.

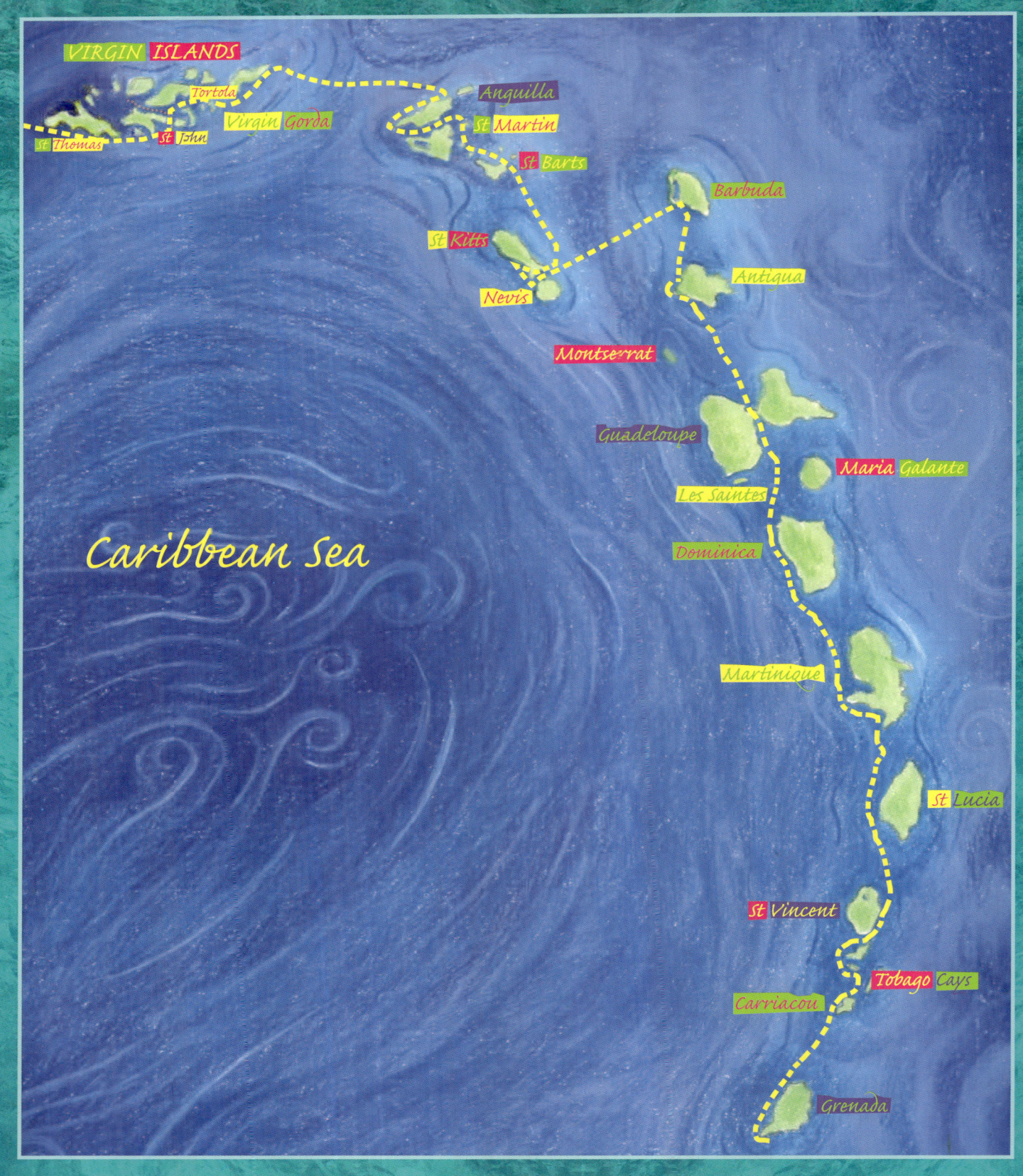

VIRGIN ISLANDS

Tortola

St John   Virgin Gorda

St Thomas

Anguilla

St Martin

St Barts

St Kitts

Nevis

Barbuda

Antigua

Montserrat

Guadeloupe

Maria Galante

Les Saintes

Dominica

Martinique

St Lucia

Caribbean Sea

St Vincent

Tobago Cays

Carriacou

Grenada

Second Season
Grenada–Virgin Islands

2008 Season, Grenada

We're now back in Grenada after five months away, two of which we spent in France where we travelled around by car exploring the wine regions. Loved our time there but would swap the highways for the seaways any day. Because the hurricane season doesn't finish for another four weeks, we are keen to get moving and will need to keep an eye on the weather, just in case of an end-of-season hurricane. The number of hurricanes in the north this year had us viewing various web weather sites on a regular basis, but thankfully none came through the southern islands where we've had *Cape Finisterre* high and dry in Prickly Bay, Grenada.

Humidity is high, temperatures are upwards of 37°C day and night, the water temperature's at 29°C, and the trade winds have not arrived yet – so we've organised for *Cape Finisterre* to be cleaned and back in the water very quickly so we can get the air-conditioner working. Not exactly ideal conditions so Ian arranges for local workers to do the antifouling and polishing. We've found Spice Island Marine to be very professional and we would recommend them to anyone thinking about leaving a yacht in their care at the end of the season.

The islands are lush green from a hot, humid and wet summer that is now ending. Grenada, just 18 km wide and 34 km long, is known as the Spice Island: nutmeg, cinnamon, cloves, cocoa, vanilla and ginger are all grown here. The population of 70,000 is mostly African with some ex-pat Brits. Despite its past political upheaval, we find it to be a relaxing tropical island set in an environmentally friendly country. We particularly enjoy a piece of roadside graffiti stating 'Thank you America for saving us', which refers to the invasion by American troops in 1983 after the ruling left wing government invited Cuban troops to assist in maintaining their hold on power. President Reagan didn't hesitate to send in troops and after their arrival everything returned to normal.

Anchored in Prickly Bay, a blue-water cove, we are surrounded by beautiful modern homes and fabulous tropical gardens full of bougainvillea and many other gorgeously colourful plants. Ian spends a few days getting the sails up and fixing a few minor areas of corrosion, then Janey, our daughter, arrives from Sydney

Ian's Cruising Notes
FLAGS
It is essential to dress your yacht correctly as it is an insult to the country you are visiting not to fly their national flag. Each island group in the Caribbean (with the exception of those belonging to France) has its own flag so a large collection is required (in our case we had 19!).

The appropriate flag must be flown from the starboard lower spreader when entering each country's waters. In some cases a yellow quarantine flag must also be flown until customs have cleared your yacht. The national ensign of the country your yacht is registered in must be flown at the stern. On *Cape Finisterre* we fly a 1 ½ yard Australian national flag and the Cruising Yacht Club of Australia burgee (triangular flag) from the port spreader.

to join us for three weeks of island hopping. When we leave we'll be heading 350 nautical miles north, to Antigua.

Meanwhile, though, we take a drive around the island during which we spot shanty houses mixed with luxury homes and a few resorts. St Georges, the capital, is steeped in island history, but while it's pretty it's not a place I'd want to be at night. High on a peninsula, overlooking yet more peninsulas and beautiful coves, we are invited by Billy, Patricia and Ian McKinney to have dinner with them at their gorgeous house from where we watch the vivid sunset. It's very tempting to stay here but we know there'll be many more magnificent sunsets to enthral us on our way north.

There's one last thing to tick off our list of things to do before we leave Grenada and that is to visit the world's first underwater sculpture park at Moliniere Bay. It's not easy to find, but at last we discover the haunting sculptures scattered on the seabed. After some time in the water they have started to become encrusted with marine life, creating artificial reefs and providing homes for fish and other sea creatures.

Soon afterwards we have another memorable experience; this one involving us coming to the rescue of a

Underwater sculpture park at Moliniere Bay (left), turtle at Tobago Cays (middle), and lobster for lunch (right)

local who'd been fishing from his boat when a large hook completely passed through his finger. Did we have wire cutters? Well, yes we did and after using them to extract the hook, the guy and his mate just carried on fishing as if nothing had happened.

Our first day sailing north is on water that's at a very pleasant sea temperature of 29°C; the breeze (what there is of it) hardly fills our sails. It's not all that refreshing, but it's great to be back at sea where keeping cool involves wearing a minimum of clothes. Our destination is Union Island in the Grenadines; our favourite cruising area in the Windward Islands. On the way we anchor off Morpion Islet, possibly the smallest island in the world, but one of the most visited among the Grenadines. It features a single thatched palm umbrella on its white sand and is surrounded by heavenly clear turquoise water. There are just too

many choices to be made in this area of white sand beaches and small islands, but if I had to choose I would return as a guest to the stunning Palm Island Resort.

The only thing to do in this heat waiting for the trade winds to arrive is swim. At Tobago Cays, one of the most beautiful natural wonders of the world, we join the turtles in the water. Saltwhistle Bay on Mayreau Island is divine and to top off a wonderful day we dine on fresh lobster cooked superbly by Ian on the barbecue. Two out of our last three meals have been lobster; and why not when it's cheaper than steak? When Ian negotiates buying it from the local fishermen, his tactic for getting it at a good price is to tell them that we're in a recession but the resulting blank expressions make it clear they have no idea what he's talking about.

Our plan this season is to sail back relatively quickly through the areas we covered during our first season to Antigua and from then on slowly through the Leeward Islands, the St Martin group, the British and US Virgins, Puerto Rico, Dominican Republic, Turks and Caicos Islands and then north through the Bahamas or along the south coast of Cuba to Central America.

Windward Islands to the Leeward Islands

It's amazing how far the arms of a hurricane can extend. Hurricane Omar, which passed through the US Virgin Islands five weeks ago, created a huge wave system, affecting the usually protected western coast of all the Windward Islands. The resulting 4-metre waves travelled 350 nautical miles and on their arrival affected some bays very badly. While we were aware that we would come across scenes of destruction, including boats that have been washed ashore, I am shocked and awed at the change from last year.

A highlight for Janey is the amazing contrast between the islands. For example, there's prestigious Mustique where rock stars and movie stars alike have holiday mansions and where we can kick back at the wonderfully peaceful Basil's Bar on the beach and then, just two hours' sail away on Bequia, we are harassed by locals and at night-time suffer from competing bar music.

On to St Lucia, a day sail, and we take the eastern side of St Vincent to find some wind. We catch, fillet, cook and eat a barracuda but miss out on the huge marlin that danced on the water then disappeared, lure and all! Interestingly, barracuda is not normally eaten due to the presence of ciguatera (a toxin found in large reef fish such as barracuda, red snapper, grouper and others), but the risk of it lessens if the fish is small and not caught within specific areas.

In every anchorage we find interesting snorkelling opportunities, e.g. peaked mountains running directly down, creating walls of fascinating life below the sea. By feeding the fish with some old bread we soon create our very own aquarium featuring the beautiful transparent blue sea all around us.

Lobster fishermen

Andrea at the helm

Piton Mountains, St Lucia

We find in Marigot Bay, St Lucia, our favourite Caribbean restaurant to date. The Rainforest Hideaway is set in a lagoon with underwater lights that create a wonderful green glow, and surrounded by mangroves and mosquitoes. The latter, uninvited and practically invisible, have been a problem on most of the islands we've visited, but thanks to mesh on all the hatches we are able to sleep relatively undisturbed but wondering why these monsters ever evolved. Rodney Bay Marina, on the north side of St Lucia and where the ARC Race finishes, has been rebuilt since we were here last year, and with the race starting again from the Canary Islands in two weeks it should be finished just in time for the next 200+ fleet of cruisers and racers.

Heading north again, we leave the humidity and warm waters behind us and start to experience some relief from the trade winds. The Martinique Channel is exciting (there's the odd little squawk from me that I'm made to feel bad about as the auto helm fights against a 35-knot gust round-up). I'm generally not impressed by waves that break under us and flick the stern, but we have a fast run so there's nothing to worry about really.

Arriving in Martinique we are astounded to see so much carnage on the shores of Anse Mitan – where we spent so much time last year – caused by the aftermath of a hurricane 400 nautical miles to the north. Le Ponton, a favourite restaurant, and the marina have gone and all that remains of the former is a shell and of the latter just the concrete piles. The beautiful beach is now covered in stones and there have been several shipwrecks on the point. It will be a long time before the marina and other buildings are replaced.

It is interesting to note that the hurricane's aftermath did not come up on a weather forecast report and while some islands including Martinique were given a three-day warning, Dominica received no warning at all. In Prince Rupert Bay, Dominica, even more boats are now stranded ashore along with the rusting ships still here after a hurricane that blew through eight years ago. How would you feel if you woke to a ship in your backyard or a mast through your balcony? It's amazing how the locals just take it in their stride, clean up, and get on with their lives.

Sitting high in a Dominica rainforest is Indigo, the Swiss Family Robinson-style art gallery and restaurant that we visited when we were here earlier. Drinking rum cocktails, we watch the sun set down the valley as birds flit in and out, including a large green native parrot – a rare sight, we're told. Marie, a French chef and artist, is married to Clem, a local, who made all the furniture out of dried branches. Janey walked 'up the garden path' to visit the long-drop toilet, as did Johnny Depp and Orlando Bloom before her when they were filming the last in the *Pirates of the Caribbean* series on this island. These two stars (among others) visited this peaceful, bohemian, wooded paradise many times.

Creole food apparently came about from an infusion of the different cultures, and varies from island to island. While I've found the local produce to be limiting at times, it is always interesting. At the moment we are in the season of avocados, bigger than you could ever imagine, and full of flavour and colour.

Ships' graveyard, Prince Rupert Bay, Dominica

Antigua

Pointe-a-Pitre, the main port on Guadeloupe, is a surprisingly pretty town with colourful shops, but our visit to the market turns out a little differently to what we expect. The yellow and red tartan-costumed transvestite with bright orange lipstick is worth a photo, but when Ian changes his mind about buying a pineapple, the mood swings and he is pelted with mangoes. We have a good laugh about it, but by the look on the locals' faces it's all happened before.

Back at the marina we are surprised at how a place can change so much at different times of the year. Our last visits took place during late winter when the sea was a beautiful blue. Now, however, it's late summer and the marina waters are brown and smelly.

We explored Basse Terre, the mountainous side of the island, including the rainforest and cascading waterfalls in the Guadeloupe National Park. The wet season is over but the rivers are torrential and a swim in fresh water provides a welcome massage.

It's still dark at our 4 am wake-up call but we have to get ourselves going or we'll miss the opportunity. Passing along the mangrove-lined river we navigate our way using the green and red navigation lights to reach the open sea on the north coast. Our 2-metre draft is pushing mud at times, but we get through in the company of four catamarans without any problems except for that brief moment at the midway point, when the lights are reversed (i.e. up until this moment the red light has been on the port side but as we are now exiting rather than entering the canal it's starboard).

All five of us are off to Antigua, 40 nautical miles away. Unbeknown to the catamarans, a race is on! Giving them a little handicap we anchor, in mid ocean, off a coral reef for breakfast. Then, under perfect sailing conditions, we overtake three of the four catamarans. Ian's excuse for not winning is that he has to slow down to haul in the 10-kg dorado we catch halfway.

Antigua is a safe haven with its two naturally enclosed harbours, English and Falmouth. At this time of year superyachts and mega motorboats are appearing every day for the beginning of the season. (Note: any young people interested in having some adventures on the sea should go get a Yacht Masters Certificate; there's plenty of work on these vessels.) The nights are long for the younger crowd. They start by meeting up at Skullduggery Bar for an Espresso Martini and then it's on to the many other bars in town.

A typical Antiguan Sunday starts at the surf beach at Half Moon Bay where cars are backed to the white sand and huge speakers beat out the reggae music. If it's a quiet day at the beach you have in mind, forget it! In the evening it's up to Shirley Heights where the steel band beats out and the rum punches flow. It's wonderful to share these experiences with Patricia, whom we met last year on Martinique and then stayed with in France. Patricia has now flown over to visit her daughter Julia, who works on a superyacht and absolutely loves the life.

Life doesn't always go to plan, though. The smell of smoke alerts us and we find the water-maker has fried some wires. Ian puts on his 'I have something to fix' look and sets about dealing with it. It's quite a learning process, but as there are no qualified marine electricians available Ian has no choice but to fix it himself.

I read somewhere that Lord Nelson said of his time in English Harbour while his ship was being rebuilt: 'When she is finished I will be under sail and leave all the mosquitoes behind'. I couldn't agree more.

It's time for our pina colada-loving daughter Janey to return home after a fabulous three weeks with us. Our last night in Antigua is spent in Jolly Harbour, after which we come face to face with the law. We'd been ashore for a cocktail and the chance to chat to friends on Skype and as we take off in our inflatable dinghy we nearly run down another big inflatable coming from the opposite direction. Evasive action on our part avoids a collision but when I call out to them, somewhat tersely, 'Where are your lights?' they reveal themselves to be the coastguard. There are six of them dressed in black, in a black inflatable with no lights, whizzing around in the harbour. They stop us and want to know who we are, and then blame us for speeding (we'd only just left the dock at a very modest 3 knots!). Apparently, this is typical behaviour; they cruise the waters in the dark looking for suspicious things. But although we think this is highly irresponsible, we don't say anything and are just happy to be sent on our way.

Cocoa Point Resort, Barbuda

West Indies – Barbuda and St Kitts

From Antigua there are many islands to visit: Montserrat (which began erupting in 1995 and continues – although on a much reduced scale – to this day so that only half of the island can be visited) to the west and St Kitts and Nevis to the northwest, but we decide to go northeast to Barbuda, 27 nautical miles away. It's particularly isolated, which is why few yachts go there, plus there are navigation difficulties. It's also not exactly in line with where we want to go, however the colony of magnificent frigate birds that breed here is a major attraction for us – and our timing is perfect for the colourful mating season.

Our last windward sail is in depths of only 22 metres, passing reefs as we go but that's the easy bit. Five miles out and all we can see is turquoise water, white beaches for miles and a very low landscape. The pilot book recommends that Cocoa Bay is a good anchorage behind a reef but when we get there we can't see a pass through the coral reef other than one at an angle. My heart is in my mouth as Ian navigates into the bay; I am on the bow spotting bombies (coral heads) with hand signals as we zigzag all the way in. We pass so close to one we could pick off a sea urchin; this kind of proximity scares the hell out of us. Once inside we have to come to terms with the fact that we can't leave until the sun is behind us (24 hours away) because that's the only time we'll be able to spot the bombies.

We find anchorage off Cocoa Point Resort – and it's paradise found. This resort was a favourite of Princess Diana's, for whom the seclusion was a welcome respite from the paparazzi. *Cape Finisterre* is the only

Heading to St Kitts (top)
Cockleshell Bay, St Kitts (middle)
Frigate birds getting ready to mate (bottom)

yacht here and as the resort is not open ours are the only footprints on the 6-km-long fine white sand beach. We soak up the atmosphere along with an orange sunset, fully aware of what a privilege it is to be here. Back on the boat and 20 nautical miles north along the coast we pass the pink sand of 11-Mile Beach and anchor. Shortly afterwards we are picked up by a guide in an open boat who takes us up the mangrove lagoon and to the frigate bird colony.

From a distance we can see the sky is black with circling birds and on our arrival we are overcome by the sight of thousands of frigate birds nesting in the mangroves. It is quite a sight with many of the male birds still in the process of attracting a mate, at which time they blow up a scarlet throat sac the size of a balloon. Those already in a relationship spend much of the time fighting over food, arguing over landing rights, who's allowed to perch where and other matters. Then there are parents sitting on eggs surrounded by baby birds being fed – it's all happening! We come in close and sit quietly; what an amazing place.

The frigate bird has a wingspan of six feet, the greatest area in proportion to their weight of any bird, and it cannot enter the sea because of the absence of natural oils in its feathers. They feed by skimming the surface and harassing other birds to give up their food and as the latter drops it, the frigate bird will swoop it up mid-air (hence their name of frigate bird or Man-o-War bird). They look awkward on land, but in the air they are very graceful as they glide in the trade winds.

Regrettably we have to leave this absolutely beautiful place. I want to stay longer but the call of the wind has Ian anticipating a fast downwind sail to St Kitts 60 nautical miles west. In 30-knot winds we are wing-and-wing with the headsail poled out, surfing off waves. Ian always has the pole attached independent of the headsail. So every time a rain squall comes through it is very easy to reef the sail back in with the pole still in place. Then, as the wind abates it's just a matter of rolling it out.

With a 3-metre swell running I am getting nervous as we approach land. We have to sail through the Narrows,

Gustavia Harbour, St Barts

the passage between Nevis and St Kitts, which is not only shallow – down to 8 metres – but is also littered with reefs. The yacht draws 2 metres and my basic calculations tell me it's going to be touch and go if we dip on a wave at the wrong time. It's amazing – in less than half a mile the sea goes from 600 to 8 metres. But thank goodness, as it turns out the swell gets less, not more.

Our first impressions of St Kitts as we arrive at the main port of Basseterre are disappointing; not least because we'd been led to believe that we could make use of the marina, which is not the case. The yachts in the outer harbour are rolling 20 degrees, which doesn't leave us much choice for the night. Persistent Ian nags the dock master into leaving his home to arrange for us to come inside the marina and tie up to the wall overnight. But we can't stay here because we're in the

way of the cruise ships that arrive here every day. Later next morning the marina staff find us another berth but it takes a few beers and a long chat about cricket (they love their cricket here, especially the Australians) before it actually happens.

We join one of the cruise ship tours, which includes a trip on the unique sugarcane railway that circumnavigates the island. Built in 1905 it is the only original cane train still in use in the Caribbean, albeit only for tourism these days as the sugarcane market collapsed with the withdrawal of subsidies by the EU.

The locals are very happy friendly people and don't appear to have a lot to worry about. Despite the fact that St Kitts was the first British Island settled in the Caribbean it does not show any benefits and without tourism it would struggle. I personally feel it's a pity

Superyachts in the marina, St Barts

that this very fertile island isn't better utilised to supply produce to its neighbouring islands.

Although our next island stop is St Barts to the north, the winds are still up so we find a sheltered bay on the southern end of St Kitts where we anchor; we are in no hurry. We spot a diver snorkelling around our yacht who then comes up with 12 huge conch shells. Still not used to the locals collecting and eating them (they're protected in Australia), we watch the meat being removed but we still have no urge to accept his offer to try one; he tells us it is even nicer to eat than lobster.

Ashore in Cockleshell Bay is the Reggae Beach Bar where we listen to our first Christmas carols to a reggae beat and where Ian soon has the locals engaged in a conversation about the history of cricket. We certainly don't have a problem passing the time here and the sign on the bar wall says it all: 'Rush Slowly'.

Ian's Cruising Notes
SECURITY AT ANCHOR

Although we are always aware of the possibility of unwanted visitors such as pirates, we don't let it rule our lives and avoid known trouble spots such as St Vincent and Venezuela. We choose not to carry a gun (we wouldn't know how to fire it!) and should intruders board, we would let them take whatever they wanted as money, phones, etc can all be replaced, but not our lives. Whenever possible we anchor where there are other boats, and at night we pull the tender up on the transom and shut the companionway. After seven years of cruising from Europe to Africa to the Caribbean and Central America (touch wood) we have never had a problem.

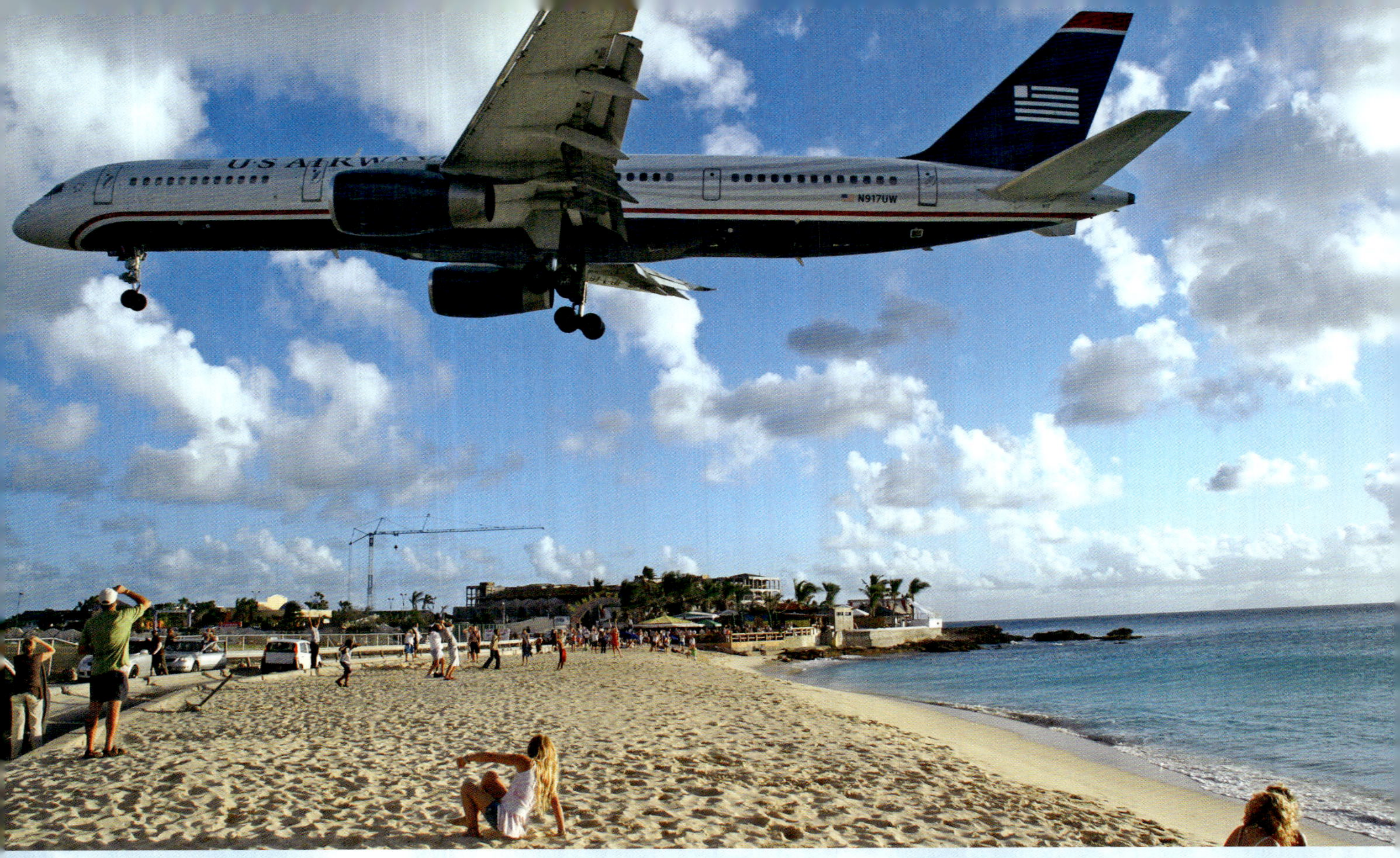
N917UW

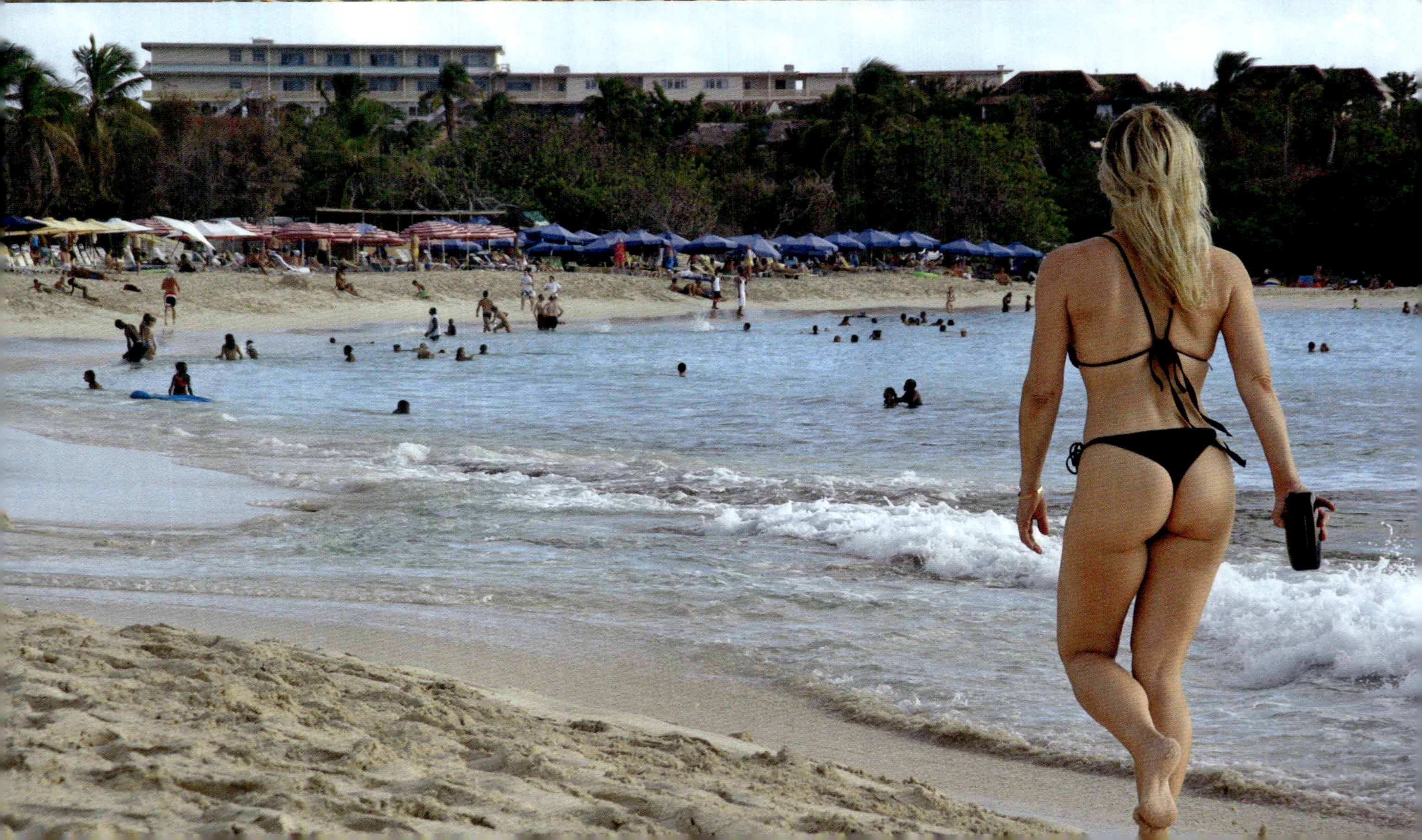

St Barts and St Martin

Then we receive a serious wake-up call. It's our last night in St Kitts, the winds have settled and we are looking forward to sailing to the luxury island of St Barts the next day. It's dark; we are anchored in a bay with no other boats around and Ian's ashore in the Reggae Beach Bar sending our last email from this island. Thinking it is time he returned, I look outside to see if the bar has closed yet – and see our dinghy floating out to sea! I do my 'fish wife call' to get Ian's attention and when he realises the dinghy is no longer there and the only way of getting back to *Cape Finisterre* is by borrowing a paddle board (there are no other boats around), he grabs it. It takes a bit for him to get the hang of the ski, including falling off once or twice, but he finally reaches the yacht (luckily he had left the computer ashore).

By this stage the dinghy is out of sight so we up anchor. After circling the bay, we head out to sea but no luck there either, so we decide it could have washed ashore on the other side of the bay. Ian wants to anchor on the lee shore and get on that surf ski thing again to look for it around the rocky shoreline. I can't convince him otherwise, so on goes the lifejacket, the line to the yacht is attached, and off he paddles towards the shore. He only gets about 15 metres under way when over he goes and I hear him say, 'I'm in trouble now!' What's happened is that his lifejacket has automatically inflated and nearly strangles him – there's too much gas in it – and the resulting bulk of it prohibits him from climbing back on the ski. Luckily he manages to let some air out of it before climbing back on the ski so I'm then able to pull him back to the yacht. Ian's not a very big man, and thanks to his years of selling and demonstrating lifejackets he knows exactly what to do in this kind of situation. For anyone else it could have been a very different outcome.

We up anchor and return to the sheltered side of the bay – without our dinghy. After numerous calls, Ian manages to get the security man at the bar on the phone who agrees to run along the shoreline in search of the dinghy while we follow his torch. Fortunately, he finds it very quickly and is able to start the motor before returning it to us. We reward him for his efforts and we are rewarded in turn by a flash of white teeth; at least someone is having a good evening.

Our next three island stops – St Barts, St Martin/Sint Maarten and Anguilla – are only miles apart but are all so different, right down to the currencies used.

St Barts (short for Saint Barthelemy and named for the brother of Christopher Columbus) is all about luxury: expensive shopping and superb restaurants on a small, unspoilt island. Everything a girl could want to celebrate 30 years of marriage can be found here. So what do we do to celebrate our anniversary? We decide there's no need to shop for diamonds or pearls, instead we hire a car and look for the perfect lunch spot. Nikki Beach Restaurant at Baie St Jean has lapping waves, white sand and breathtaking turquoise waters. Then, for our evening meal on this special day we choose Caviar Bar where we relax on cushions and drink champagne. The only things missing are our friends, family and readers of our blog – love to you all, and thank you for being part of our lives!

Gustavia is the main port/town on St Barts and it has just about every major fashion house (think Gucci, Dior, etc) represented along with Rolex, Cartier and the like. The place will be wall-to-wall with assorted superyachts by Christmas but it's only a small port, so yachts like ours anchor out, which can be a problem if you're too far out with no protection against the big swell.

We're impressed by the sky-blue colour of the very clear and very inviting waters surrounding this island. Initially settled by the French, then the Swedes, St Barts is now back in the hands of the French and the local architecture is an interesting mixture of both cultures. When the tourism industry first got under way in the 1960s, the locals got on board and have never looked back.

Around the corner is Anse de Colombier, a nature reserve bay. From now on laid moorings will become more frequent to protect the ocean floor from dragging anchors. Turtles returning to the surface for air become a frequent sight alongside our yacht. A storm to the north has created a large swell so after another uncomfortable night in rolling seas we set sail to the island of St Martin. We have a fast 25-nautical-mile reach to enter

Christmas lunch, Sint Maarten

on the French side; apparently there's less bureaucracy to deal with here than on the Dutch side.

For the last 350 years the island has been divided between the French and the Dutch and is known both as St Martin and Sint Maarten, depending on which side you are visiting. Its inland water, Simpson Lagoon, can only be entered when the bridges that cross it are lifted. And since we have come in on the French side, our yacht must stay on their half of the waterway – although in our dinghy we are free to go anywhere without our passports. Being in the lagoon has its advantages; the main one being shelter as it has been very windy (at this time of year this is known as the Christmas winds). It will be nice not to have to worry about that aspect for a while.

Ashore it's all very commercial what with the international airport and duty-free shops everywhere.

There is also a large number of nautical establishments that service all the marinas which are full of every kind of boat imaginable. Ian has a list of 'fix it', 'fill it' or 'replace it' to keep him busy.

Everywhere we go we always look out for fellow New Zealanders or Australians and here in the lagoon we spy *Sumatra*, a Swan 48 flying an Aussie flag. Shane Diethelm, a CYCA (Cruising Yacht Club of Australia) Youth Academy sailor with his CYCA member family on board (parents Basil and Angela, and brother Tristan) has just sailed down from the USA.

Christmas and New Year in St Martin

The combination of Christmas, Caribbean and cruising has become problematic. Christmas winds of 35 knots, big waves up to 4 metres and rain for the last three days means we are unable to leave the lagoon so we just have to make the most of it. An Australian boat anchors beside us and we quickly get to know Peter and Nanni from Melbourne who are cruising in *Joules*, their Island Packet 40-footer. Turtle Pier Bar is the preferred location for cruisers to get together on Christmas Eve, and it's here that we meet New Zealanders Lynette and Rene Rasing who left Tauranga three and a half years ago to cruise the world. In true Kiwi style, they issue an invitation to join them for Christmas Day lunch on the dock.

We enjoy a Christmas Eve turkey dinner and prawn cocktail at Jimbo's with Peter and Nanni and then a barbecue lunch followed by pavlova and trifle the next day – a delicious if unplanned Christmas. We're all sailing in different directions and although we may never meet again we stay in touch by email.

Being stuck here in the lagoon has its advantages for Ian. Parts and repair facilities in Simpson Lagoon are excellent and as a result of the duty-free shopping in Philipsburg, we now have a DVD player that will work anywhere. The latest movies (sold to us as 'original copy,

mon') keep us entertained when it's too wet to go ashore. Interestingly, these highly illegal copies actually feature copyright warnings!

More Australians anchor near us; Cameron Hunter from Melbourne has just crossed the Atlantic in his Amel 54 *Reborn V*. He read my first book, *Letters from the Med*, two years ago, after which he sold his business, bought a yacht and with his wife and three young children sailed the Med themselves and are now sailing the Caribbean. It's great to see a young family having such wonderful adventures together.

Suddenly the sunshine returns, the trade winds settle and we head off in a rental car to explore some of St Martin's beautiful beaches. The island is seven miles long and seven miles wide so it doesn't take too long. As we leisurely walk past the colourful umbrellas dotting the white sands of Orient Beach, I spot a male figure wearing nothing but a sun hat. Rolf Harris' song 'Jake the Peg' instantly comes to mind as we notice the size of what he is proudly showing off. We quickly make our exit as we become aware of the signs around us

Baie St Jean, St Martin

Ile Pinel, St Martin (top)

New Year's Eve,
Anse Marcel

St Martin

banning clothes and cameras. We have no desire for sunburnt scrotums, tits or other bits.

It's New Year's Eve and Anse Marcel is the perfect setting in which to celebrate: luxury resort, space lighting, music and fireworks. But I discover that a long flowing dress and a dinghy are not necessarily a compatible combination. All dolled up, I miss my footing to the dock and fall into the harbour. If it was the end of the night and I'd had a drink or two I might have seen the funny side of it but as the night has just started I'm not very impressed. But it all comes right and after a change of clothes, the rest of the night is all glamour. Welcome 2009.

We spend New Year's Day in calm blue waters and round the top of St Martin to Ile Pinel. A sand peninsula, azure seas, beautiful people, lobster for lunch – what more could you want for a Caribbean Christmas?

Meeting up with a number of American cruisers and getting information about where we are headed is exciting. After many changes we almost have a plan on our direction for the rest of the season. Our friends back in Australia keep saying 'don't come home', so we don't plan on it.

Happy New Year—Anguilla

At latitude 18° north and longitude 63° west, the low-lying Anguilla is the most northerly of the Leeward Islands and on the outermost extremity of the arc of the Caribbean Islands. Only 8 nautical miles to the north of St Martin, it is a very easy passage. The island is in the shape of an eel, hence it being named as such by Columbus (*anguilla* is Spanish for eel). From here on we'll be sailing west with trade winds from astern; nothing too difficult.

Ian's Cruising Notes
SAFETY GEAR

Our safety gear includes an eight-man ISO Ocean life raft for 24 hours plus duration that comes in a soft pack and is stowed for easy access in a specially designed locker on the transom of the yacht. Also in this locker is our grab bag that contains extra water, baked beans, can opener, barley sugars, glow sticks and torches. Once activated, our EPIRBs will allow the relevant authorities to locate us within 24 hours.

Each passenger has their own inflatable lifejacket with built-in harness, strobe light and personal 406 EPIRB. There is also a horseshoe life buoy with drogue and whistle, inflatable danbouy and a life sling mounted on the pushpit.

The deck has 'jackstays' running down either side for attaching the safety line of our harnesses. We have a rule that during night sailing the person on watch must wear their lifejacket and harness at all times. And if alone on deck, that person should not leave the cockpit.

A coral reef that extends for miles protects Anguilla from the Atlantic waves. Inside the reef the water is gorgeously coloured ranging from aquamarine to sapphire to turquoise. Then there are the whiter than white fine sand beaches. Ashore there are plenty of luxury hotels and good restaurants but that's where the impression of paradise ends. Perhaps the development here has been too fast and the infrastructure and local needs forgotten in the rush.

Since 1980 Anguilla has been a separate British dependency (it was first colonised by English settlers in 1650 and then, along with St Kitts and Nevis 75 nautical miles south, was incorporated into a single British dependency in the early nineteenth century).

Hurricane Omar, which passed through the Caribbean in October 2008, tracked through the island, but no one complains; they just rebuild and move on. We heard that the beach in Road Bay was littered with yachts and fishing boats after Omar but the soft sand surrounding the bay made it relatively easy for them all to be dragged off.

Road Bay Harbour is one of the nicest harbours and there is no charge to anchor here. When visiting other bays and islands offshore we need to buy a daily permit at a cost of US$50 and although some cruisers get upset about paying, we're not bothered – especially when the money goes towards protection of the coral and sea life.

We spend a couple of days here and have to revisit Shoal Beach to ensure we hadn't dreamed our experience there. I'd highly recommend it for anyone seeking tranquillity to heal the mind, body or soul. It would have to be one of the nicest beaches I have ever seen – all wrapped in blue, the air is clear and breezy, the sky is bright and the water inviting. As Chief Seattle famously said back in the 1850s, 'Take nothing but memories, leave nothing but footprints.'

Anguilla is our departing point for the British Virgin Islands, 80 nautical miles to the west. For us it's a day sail as we can average eight knots in a good wind. There are two weather websites that we check regularly. One is www.windguru.com, used mainly by surfers and kiteboarders because it shows the windiest places (this one suits me because at a quick glance I can get wind strength, direction and most important wave height and direction). Ian prefers www.buoyweather.com, which shows what's going on in the whole area. At the moment we are looking for wind so we don't burn diesel fuel, even though it is cheap at US.83c a litre. Saturday shows the perfect picture with just enough wind to keep Ian happy and a following 2-metre wave height, which makes me happy.

Before leaving we enjoy a day trip sailing to Prickly Pear Island, which was declared a national park in 1988. It's a paradise of coral and crystal-clear water and has only two beach bars ashore.

Saturday has arrived and as dawn breaks at 5.30 am the anchor is up, the mainsail is hoisted but then a tropical storm passes over. We take a quick

Road Bay, Anguilla

glance to ensure we clear the very low Sandy Island to the north as visibility is nil, but a beautiful day follows and by 11 am we are halfway to our next destination. Then zingggg! Suddenly our forgotten fishing line demands our attention. We haul our catch aboard and out come the fish books. Soon we identify it as a 10-kg wahoo, one of the fastest fish in the sea and a first for us. Better still, we can eat it as it's not a species known to carry any toxins such as *ciguatera*. According to the locals in this part of the world, there are two methods of finding out if a fish is poisonous. The first involves ants – apparently they won't go near a poisonous fish – but I don't have any ants on board. The second is to place a slice of potato on the flesh; if it goes black then the fish is poisonous. My own theory is – if in doubt let it go.

But the wahoo does have a small win; when flicking the fish into the inflatable dinghy that is always hauled up on the transom when we're sailing, the hook manages to puncture one of the tubes and it deflates very quickly. Just another repair job when we anchor.

Both weather sites prove to be correct and we have a perfect crossing, sailing all the way and all up taking nine hours.

We pass Necker Island, Richard Branson's private paradise island complete with imitation palms on the small sand cay in the lagoon. The air throbs with the sound of helicopters coming and going from the superyachts that are anchored all around.

We are going to be here for over six weeks so there's plenty of time to explore the many beautiful and lush islands of the British Virgin Islands (BVIs), which many cruisers consider equal in beauty to the Ionian Islands of Greece.

The Baths, Virgin Gorda, British Virgin Islands

British Virgin Islands

An area of approximately 50 islands, the British Virgin Islands are a sailor's fantasy. With a constant wind of 15–25 knots, we can go where it takes us. Pirates, mostly English, once ruled these islands, hiding in the secluded bays and burying their treasure ashore. Numerous bays and channels are named after Sir Francis Drake, a well-known pirate who, in our school days, we were all led to believe was an English hero. The pirates would conveniently position themselves in remote coves around the islands in order to raid the Spanish galleons returning to Europe loaded with all the gold and silver they themselves had stolen from the Indians of South and Central America.

Now charter yachts are here in their hundreds (we have never seen so many in one place) and no doubt some of these experience the odd mutiny on board.

Pauline Christie from Sydney joins us, and after all the formalities of checking in at Spanish Harbour on Virgin Gorda – the third-largest of the BVIs – are complete we take a taxi to The Baths, one of the most interesting geological attractions – and a byproduct of the island's volcanic or gins – in the eastern Caribbean. Huge granite boulders lie separately and in piles on the beach, the latter creating tunnels and caves.

The coral atoll of Anegada, 14 nautical miles to the north, is flat with a reef that extends for miles and which is littered with wrecks; it's claimed over 300 vessels so far. 'We won't be going there' is my first thought, but as it happens we do and it's a wonderful sail in shallow but royal blue seas all the way. There is only one entrance through the reef which, thank goodness, is marked by buoys (without them our electronic chart would have put us on the reef). The lagoon is open to all weather and the wind is menacing at anchor, especially with over 40 charter yachts all squeezed into a very small area. No one minds; it's a beautiful place to be. Anegada is famous for its big lobster, pink flamingos and beautiful beaches with snorkelling inside the reef on the northern coast. Although one of the biggest islands, it has a population of only 250.

Jimmy Buffett, the well-known singer/guitarist famous for 'Margaritaville' and 'Cheeseburger in Paradise', cruises these waters but no one knows when he might appear at a bar and put on an impromptu show. We find out later that the big 100-ft motor yacht at the entrance to the bay was his and he'd come ashore that night and performed unannounced at the Anegada Reef Bar while we sat on board drinking Kahlua.

We return to anchor in North Sound, Virgin Gorda, where Sir Francis Drake used to hide. The sound, which becomes our base for a few nights, is very large and is probably the best shelter – whatever the weather – in all the Virgins. Close by are two huge mega-yachts, each complete with a helicopter, both owned by Microsoft

directors. Maybe we should invite them across to sort out our Vista problems! Ashore is the Bitter End Resort, the bars of which are well known to the visiting yachties thanks to a special rum-based alcoholic drink unique to the BVIs known as a Painkiller. Add four parts pineapple juice and one each of orange juice and cream of coconut to however much rum you want, then grate fresh nutmeg on top.

Then we find paradise in a horseshoe bay protected by a reef, a resort ashore but room for only one boat. Ian is never one to be on the outside so in we go with clearance of only 25 cm below the keel! Paradise, or Little Dix Bay on the west side of Virgin Gorda, becomes home for three days. Pauline and I snorkel among turtles, stingrays and a few coral fish on the largely dead reef. The coral is disappointing after what we've seen in the Pacific Ocean (but let's keep that a secret). Ashore iguanas wander the paths and on the water pelicans keep us amused as they dive for fish, some even in

Anegada Reef Bar, British Virgin Islands

We settle for the night off Marina Cay, famous for the best-selling book and movie Our Virgin Island, which is about the young English couple that purchased the island in the 1940s for $60.

Little Dix Bay Resort, British Virgin Islands (top)
Marina Cay, Tortola Island (bottom left)
Permanent resident, Pirates Beach Bar, Marina Cay (bottom right)

unison. Ian becomes a hero, thanks to his laser sailing school days, when a guest at the resort needs rescuing. The boom hit the 85-year-old's head while gybing and dumped him onto the reef.

We almost take on local status with all our dining ashore and frequenting of the bars. Prices, however, are keeping us on the slim side as well as sober, but we feel sorry for the 19 per cent occupancy rate – and this is high season – which appears to be the norm for resorts and charter companies just now.

Regulars tell us about the best snorkelling areas so off we sail to explore the small islands north of Tortola. They are the best we have seen so far in the Virgins with their beautiful coloured fish and fan coral. We settle for the night off Marina Cay, famous for the best-selling book and movie *Our Virgin Island*, which is about the young English couple that purchased the island in the 1940s for $60. The bar on the island is now famous for its singing pirate – he's attracted quite a following of cruisers over time and they anchor here year after year to enjoy his lyrical rolling 'rrrrrrrrrrrrs' and the copious quantities of Pusser's (the original navy rum, which according to local legend was used to preserve Nelson's body) that he gives away. Needless to say, we have a great time enjoying his hospitality.

Peter and Norman Islands, British Virgins

Let me take you through a typical day in the BVIs. We wake in Great Harbour, Peter Island, in crystal-clear water, but a swim before breakfast is out of the question because the day before I'd spotted a large fish looking suspiciously like a shark to me that came to greet us as we anchored. It's now taken up residence under the yacht and peers at me every time I try to enter the water. My answer to the problem is to send Ian in first. By mid morning we are swimming side by side, but my eyes never leave it.

Then, looking very official with her white ensign flags flying, *Leander* arrives in the bay. Last year Prince Charles and Camilla chartered this beautiful superyacht and we wonder who we might see on board this time.

Now it's time to head upwind for 3 miles to Salt Island,

where the 310-ft Royal Mail Ship *Rhone* went down in 1867. The steam ship was anchored safely in Great Bay when an out-of-season hurricane hit without warning. Trying to flee the islands she hit the southwest end of Salt Island, broke in two and sank, taking 124 lives. Snorkelling below the surface we see the wreck, a sight that neither of us will ever forget. Now a leading Caribbean wreck dive site in crystal-clear water, the skeletal remains of the ship rest only metres from the rock that caused the fatal wreck. We note the centre drive shaft that extends out to deeper waters with the ribs reaching out to the sides. The propeller is visible and the huge rudder lies on its side as if still in action. As I float motionless above, I imagine the sound of her hitting the rock, the screams of the people and the roar of the hurricane. The result of a tragedy in such a beautiful place now forms a habitat for marine life.

Just half a mile to the north of Peter Island is the infamous 'Dead Chest Cay', so-named because it resembles a coffin or, in pirate talk, a Dead Chest. It is supposedly the place where the infamous pirate who went by the name of Blackbeard marooned 15 of his crew with only a bottle of rum. None survived, although a few tried swimming half a mile to the beautiful bay on Peter Island which now bears the same name. The rhyme to mark the event, 'Yo-ho-ho and a bottle of rum!' still lives on. Both the book *Treasure Island* and the movie *Pirates of the Caribbean* contain references to this little cay.

With rolled-out headsail we sail to Norman Island, made famous by Robert Louis Stevenson's book *Treasure Island*. Snorkelling in the pristine water in the three pirate caves each populated with colourful tropical fish, we come away with a different kind of treasure – stunning visual sights to treasure in our memories. The island is basically uninhabited, apart from the 70 yachts taking up the moorings in Bight Bay, and of course the family that runs Pirates Beach Bar during the season. Live music and a few drinks at the bar bring a happy ending to yet another cruising day.

Later that night, as Ian and I lie on the foredeck listening to the steel band still going strong ashore, we gaze at the bright galaxy of stars and imagine what it was like back in the days when piracy was rife throughout the islands.

Norman Island   *Colourful fish are everywhere in the Caribbean*

Another day passes. We are now back on Peter Island and spend a few days tied stern to the shore. We admire the cacti in their various forms that are growing on the cliffs and the aloe vera on the shoreline. Pelicans entertain us on a regular basis and we are without contact with the world. Who cares?

It is hard to believe that we still have over 1750 nautical miles to sail, all with the trade winds behind us. It will be new territory for us, covering several countries not normally visited by cruising yachts.

While we are here, an ongoing mystery is solved. The light banging we sometimes hear against the hull at night is caused by none other than the occasional turtle drifting into the side of our yacht. It is great to see so many of these beautiful creatures in the sea.

We are noticing the days getting longer and the winter passing. Winter? What winter?

British Virgin—US Virgin Islands

As a very popular cruising ground the BVIs attract a lot of attention and now I can see why. For cruising purposes, they really are the best in the Caribbean.

Road Harbour, the main port on the largest island of Tortola has three cruise ships arriving every day but for us the only reason to visit is to provision. Leaving Road Harbour under sail, Ian sights a floating fender and throws my way a 'man overboard' drill; I have to pick it up or at least come near it. In my mind I'm constantly going through the motions in my mind in case such an incident should happen. But now I steer the yacht into the wind, roll up the headsail and let the main flap. The fender is now in front of me and with the motor on I am able to steer to it. Courtesy of a charter company, Ian is now the owner of a large fender that will come in handy when we pass through the Panama Canal (and I will get my reward later!).

Soper's Hole, a very deep sheltered bay on the west end of Tortola, is our anchorage for one night. The marina village ashore, built in Creole style, is the home of Voyage Charters, a company that operates a fleet of large catamarans. Cane Garden Bay on the northwestern side is generally recognised as the pick of the beaches on Tortola. Protected by a dangerous reef it offers excellent shelter off the white sand beach lined with coconut palms and beach bars all overlooked by the lush mountain behind. One of the bars is Quito's where Quito and his live band keep us entertained with reggae until daybreak. While sitting at the bar we meet Doug and Linda Jones from the USA who live here for four months each year. They invite us to their beautiful mountaintop home the next night, where we watch the sun set over Sir Francis Drake Channel and the US Virgin Islands. On a clear day they can see as far as Puerto Rico. Ian is sold on it as a great spot.

Jost van Dyke, named after a Dutch pirate, is our last island and it is photographic heaven: a kaleidoscope of colours and world famous for its white beaches and beach bars including Foxy's, One Love and Soggy Dollar. All day long it is one big beach party with great live entertainment (no need to tell you how the 'soggy dollar' came about, is there?). This is one of our favourite islands and after several days we are sad to leave.

Now it's time to cross the watery border to the USA, just seven miles away and where 'Big Brother' is waiting for us. Before we left Sydney we had to obtain a B1/B2 visa, which requires an eye photo (i.e. the iris is scanned) and fingerprints; this is because we are entering on our own boat and not on a commercial vessel. Not many non-US cruisers bother to go to the US Virgins due to this kind of restriction and on our arrival we are terrified that we may have got some paperwork wrong. But considering all the hassles to get the correct visa, we are treated really casually on entry. What an anticlimax! But our papers are in order, we are stamped in for six months and that is that – welcome to the USA.

Cane Garden Bay, Tortola Island

Jost van Dyke Island

The US Virgins comprise three main islands: St Johns, which is nearly 60 per cent national park (courtesy of the Rockefeller family); St Thomas, the capital full of resorts; and St Croix, 35 nautical miles to the south. The last one is not on our radar because it's mainly industrial.

On St John we discover Cruz Bay Village to be a delight. It has a feeling of great peacefulness, which was not the case during the Danish occupation of the eighteenth and nineteenth centuries when 109 plantations of sugar cane were in operation. For 150 years slaves on these islands were treated incredibly badly by the Danes. A rebellion by the slaves against the white owners in 1733 lasted six months until crushed with the assistance of the French. While it didn't bring an end to slavery, it did at least highlight the conditions, especially on this island. Eventually the islands were sold to the USA in 1917.

With *Finisterre* anchored in Leinster Bay we walk to the ruins of Annaberg Sugar Mill plantation, now open to the public and a visual reminder of the harsh conditions endured by the slaves. Their duties included clearing steep hillsides, then terracing them before planting them with cane - all in extreme heat. Then they had to tend fires, which cooked the juice from the crushed cane that eventually became sugar. After a very long day outdoors the slaves then had to tend to their own gardens if they were going to have anything to eat. Unsurprisingly, the survival rate on the islands was only seven years. All this for the production of sugar, molasses and rum, shipped out to sweeten Europe's tooth.

On a lighter note I read an article about President Richard Nixon coming here for a holiday many years ago. You can imagine the security that was in place – this was at the time of the bombing of Cambodia. Some young

Jost van Dyke Island is famous for its beach bars

hippies anchored their boat in the bay not far from his hotel and hoisted a sail with an anti-war slogan painted on it in blood red. Nixon was not amused, especially as the security detail had already been in place for some time before he even arrived. I hear those same hippies are still here in Coral Bay, living on the same old yachts, although we haven't actually seen them for ourselves.

Inner Vision, a successful local reggae band, is playing ashore. It's fantastic; there is just so much talent around that we are never without live music.

Every bay on St John has a number of moorings, the use of which is compulsory and at a cost of US$15 per night. Although a token amount, the money raised goes towards protecting and helping rejuvenate the sea grass and coral in the area.

We move on to St Thomas and its capital, Charlotte Amalie. It's very commercial and everything is aimed at attracting tourist dollars, and ideally more cruise ships. One could easily confuse Larry Ellison's personal 280-ft superyacht *Rising Sun* with one of the cruise ships that take up most of the marina. However, a big swell is running from the north so at least it's shelter for a few days. Most of the bars, restaurants and luxury shops are slow so the recession must be starting to affect all the islands.

Amid all the synthetic luxury we enjoy a precious moment while we're in the dinghy on our way to shore. A large stingray flies through the air, showing us his white underbelly, then hits the surface. The amazing thing is that he does it four times. No time for photos though but afterwards we tell ourselves how lucky we are that he didn't actually land on board – that could have been a bit of a problem!

Time to prepare for moving on to the Spanish Virgin Islands, only 20 nautical miles to the west.

Remains of the slave era, St John, US Virgin Islands   *Culebra, Spanish Virgin Islands*

Spanish Virgin Islands

Now that we're about to spend some time in the Spanish Virgin Islands (SVI), let me give you some background. Geographically part of the Virgin Islands chain, this group is part of the Commonwealth of Puerto Rico. The two principal islands are Culebra and Vieques, 15 and 6 nautical miles respectively off the eastern coast of Puerto Rico. But although US territory the SVI are politically and culturally distinct from the territory of the Virgin Islands of the United States (more commonly known as the US Virgin Islands) that are east of the SVI.

They're very Spanish in many ways (not surprising given that Puerto Rico belonged to Spain until 1898) including language and food – all of which makes a refreshing change – and are much as you might imagine the Caribbean to have been like 30 years ago. Things are generally pretty quiet, i.e. until the weekend when the Puerto Ricans charge out to sea in their big stink boats.

Vieques, the larger of the two islands, has only just opened up to the public as it was a military training ground for the USA until quite recently. Military evidence is apparent here and there and we only hope that we don't put an anchor down on an unexploded bomb. So many beautiful beaches dot the islands that it's hard to imagine all the war games that must have gone on here.

We leave via Magen's Bay, supposedly one of the top 10 beaches in the Caribbean (but we have seen many that rate higher), on the north coast of the small island of St Thomas to sail the 20 nautical miles to Culebra in frisky winds. By the time we get there it is blowing 30 knots; we are under full sail and Ian is in his element, not wanting this great sail to come to an end. There's a narrow channel to be navigated through the reef, coral heads are showing only metres away and we are sailing at 9 knots. Thankfully the channel is well marked with green and red buoys and Ian rounds them, pilot book in one hand, as he glances at the chart plotter and fiddles with sails. Some people might think this is exciting, but

it's a nerve-racking experience for me. Soon, though, we are safely anchored off the town of Dewey in Ensenada Honda, the largest harbour on the island, where I enjoy my well-deserved rum cocktail.

Our stay here is a lot longer than we planned as the winds increase, but the Louis Vuitton Pacific Series being sailed in New Zealand is keeping us entertained. More often than not, we get wireless Internet connection on board and the latest aerial certainly makes life easier. We've just purchased for US$80 the latest model (High-Power IEEE 802.11b/g AP dongle) that can pick up sites over 4 km away in the town of Dewey. Every yacht club seems to offer a free wireless service, even those operating out of tiny shacks.

Leaving the shelter of the reef where we've been moored for the last little while we sail to the island of Vieques where we spot our first whales. As we are now entering whale territory we expect to see many more as we sail northwest. Winds prevent us from visiting Puerto Mosquito, a bioluminescent bay located on the southern shore of Vieques. We will return next week and try again when there's no moon – apparently the best time to go.

Anchoring off the village of Esperanza, we go ashore to enjoy some Spanish music that's played in the local bars, but we end up listening to some excellent guitar playing from Kiwi Kim, all the way from Dunedin, New Zealand.

In the process of launching the dinghy to motor back to the yacht we experience an unfortunate incident when two large rocks are thrown at us, both of them luckily landing short and hitting the water. There's a lot of anti-American sentiment here – we must start wearing Aussie or Kiwi colours to show where we are from.

It's time to provision again so we head for mainland Puerto Rico and anchor in the shelter of Isleta Marina (a small island) off the city of Fajardo. But after taking the ferry ashore a culture shock awaits us: the city is dirty, scruffy and its huge supermarkets are full of American goods. Fast food outlets dominate the area and we're hoping we will find the south coast a lot more interesting. Despite this disappointing visit, I must say we are enjoying wonderful sailing wherever we go with hardly any motoring, a real pleasure even when it is hard on the wind.

Providenciales

Turks & Caicos Islands

Lt Inagua Is

Grand Turk

Gt Inagua Is

CUBA

Guantanamo Bay

Windward Passage

Puerto Rico Trench

Luperon

HAITI

DOMINICAN REPUBLIC

San Juan

Vieques

Santo Domingo

PUERTO RICO

Ponce

Boquerón

Caribbean Sea

Aruba

Bonaire

Curaçao

COLOMBIA

VENEZUELA

Second Season
Virgin Islands—Cuba

shops selling fruit at Bahia de Luperon, Dominican Republic

Puerto Rico

Joining us this week are Geordie and Patricia Burnett-Stuart whom we met in Martinique last year. Arriving from cold Europe, they enjoy a welcome swim off the island of Palominos before we sail south back to the Spanish Virgin Island of Vieques.

A return visit to Mosquito Bay is the reason we are back here and just as the sun is setting we are picked up from Esperanza by a minivan towing 20 canoes. Mosquito Bay looks nothing special during the day, but at night it becomes one of the wonders of the world. Wearing only swimsuits on this pitch-black night, we paddle out to the middle of the bay on the canoes, trying as we go not to lose contact with our group. Almost instantly we see the fish below dart about in the luminescent water; then the paddle and the canoe itself cause a glowing trail. When we reach the middle of the bay, we swim. Stirring up the sea to encourage the luminescent effect is amazing and it's fascinating to watch what looks like thousands of sparkling diamonds rolling off our skin. This magical effect is caused by countless microscopic organisms known as dinoflagellates that release energy in the form of light, much the way fireflies do, at the slightest disturbance. It's generally thought that the ability of these tiny creatures to glow is as a result of a chemical reaction to warn away predators.

It's a very fragile ecosystem here and canoes are the favoured method of transportation since it's been discovered that the pollution from outboard motors was killing the organisms.

As we enjoy the warm water I'm reminded of the time in New Zealand when we were sailing north past a reef on a dark night. Suddenly a couple of dolphins charged towards the yacht, their bodies outlined in sparkling luminescence; it scared the hell out of me! And yes for those who really want to know, you sometimes see a similar effect when you flush the head on a boat.

One evening we eat a very nice dinner at el Quenepo in Esperanza but as Ian gets into the dinghy to go back to the yacht later that night he spots a local with a rock in his hand. After Ian gives him a filthy stare, the man abandons his intentions.

Our sail halfway along the southern coast of Puerto Rico is in glorious blue sea with foaming white waves building behind us. An exhilarating 55-nautical-mile ride in a 25-knot easterly takes us to Bahia de Jobos, a hurricane hole behind a coral reef and many mangrove-covered cays. Entering is not for the faint-hearted as we surf in between the waves, but once inside it's flat calm even though we can still hear the roar of the waves crashing on the coral.

We venture out the next morning to discover a maze of coral cays, some above the water and some just below – thank goodness for GPS. Coffin Island (Isla

Small wooden houses and friendly children at Bahía de Luperón

de Muertos), once a pirate haven, is a beautiful and typical Caribbean island, i.e. blue water, white sand, palm trees, and of course a resort. But the strong winds make anchoring uncomfortable and after a lobster lunch we sail onto Ponce, the main port on this coast and the second-largest city on Puerto Rico. Ponce was first settled in the 1500s and is named after the Spanish Governor of the time, Ponce de Leon.

A day in downtown Ponce allows us to see the beautiful facades and classical Spanish architecture, all of which have been well preserved. In the Plaza Las Delicias we find grand fountains overshadowed by ficus trees and the silver-domed Cathedral of Our Lady of Guadaloupe. Outside the city it's all fast highways and fast food, very American. It's interesting that while they can't fix the internet service, they can build another hamburger outlet.

So far many places ashore have been disappointing, but the natural scenery and sailing have been superb. But I'm not so sure that this will be the case for those sailing in the other direction as most are holed up in the mangroves waiting for the winds to abate.

Geordie and Patricia depart and we take advantage of the huge Puerto Rican supermarkets to restock for the voyage ahead to Cuba before Ian and I sail down the coast to Gilligan's Island Nature Reserve. Then it's on to La Paguera where weekend poled homes are built out over the mangroves in the water; most have a fishing

boat tied to the veranda or moored in the boat-port to the side.

All along this coast manatees (big blubbery creatures that are somewhere between a sunfish and a giant seal) feed off the sea grass around the mangroves. We've been advised to take care to avoid them as they are protected but I catch sight of one submerging.

Boqueron on the southern end of the west coast is our last port of call before departing for the Dominican Republic. This has to be the nicest village we have visited in Puerto Rico: we appreciate the pretty cottages and the street vendors selling fresh oysters in their shells. A speciality of the bay, they are very similar to Sydney rock oysters and are absolutely delicious.

Dominican Republic

The Mona Passage, an 30-nautical-mile strait between Puerto Rico and the Dominican Republic, is a very unpredictable stretch of water renowned for its strong currents. During the Spanish occupation the strait was a main passage for the Spanish galleons sailing back to Spain full of bullion. Our destination is Luperon, 240 nautical miles west along the north coast of the Dominican Republic. The total sailing distance means two nights and one day at sea, making it our first overnight passage since crossing the Atlantic in 2007.

We are now in the Caribbean's Greater Antilles comprising Puerto Rico, Hispaniola (the Haiti and the

Ian's Cruising Notes
TENDER STORAGE

Davits on the transom are handy but I devised my own system that has worked well for us for many years and which allows us to haul up the tender with the outboard still in place. Our system allows for this to be done quickly and single-handedly, but the tender has to be able to lay one hull along the boarding platform. It uses two block and tackle systems with a purchase of four simple open hooks attached to the side of the dinghy at the bow and stern and then attached to the pushpit. By lifting the closest side up onto the boarding platform the dinghy is easily raised by hauling in on both lines, which are attached to the far side of the tender. We even sail with it like this but we tie it down in the event a following wave gets underneath.

Note: Our lightweight tender has a rigid bottom and a folding transom. It fits into a low profile bag that can be lashed to the deck. We chose to fit it with a 2HP 6-cylinder outboard as they are easier to clean when they end up in the sea, which is not uncommon.

Dominican Republic), Cuba and Jamaica. The Dominican Republic (DR) port entry is a bureaucratic nightmare as well as being quite expensive. Every port in DR requires re-entry and given our time frame this limits our choices.

Sailing past the Samana Peninsula on the northeastern corner of the DR we note mountain ranges covered in thousands of coconut palms, and some of the most beautiful beachfronts in the Caribbean; the blue waters lap at the white sand leading up to the coconut palms presided over by the lush green mountains. As the sun sets we are gifted with the magnificent sight of humpback whales and their calves spouting around us. This is whale-breeding territory and the great mammals travel thousands of miles from the Arctic to come here for the winter months. I love to see them during the day, but prefer not to think about them at night other than hope they are not in our path. During our first night out I become aware of a pretty unpleasant salty smell to weather (i.e. windward) of us and after I've established that Ian has not been indiscreet, I realise that a whale has just spouted not very far away. For some reason the seawater spouted by whales has a stale, salty smell. A bit close for comfort!

The only dilemma on this particular passage is the failure of the autopilot, a piece of equipment that is effectively our third crew member. Its failure can make life very difficult, especially at night and when there are only two of us on board. What's happened is that the bolt attaching the pilot arm to the rudderstock had sheared off. However, Ian manages to repair it although it's not an easy job in the confused seas. It's good to know those spares can come in handy after all!

After 38 hours at sea we enter Bahia de Luperon at daybreak. We navigate our way through a very narrow entrance and over a shallow bar that opens up to a mangrove-surrounded lagoon; the perfect hurricane hole. In fact it's probably the best in the Caribbean for those wanting to live aboard their yacht during the hurricane season. Inside at any one time are around 100 yachts; some are just passing through, some staying for a few days and others staying for two years. I suspect that many of the cruisers that arrive here after coming south from the Bahamas become so secure in this sheltered harbour that they are too frightened to continue further east or south. We rename it 'Chicken Harbour'.

It takes five uniformed men: customs, immigration, agriculture, tourism and port control to complete the entry formalities, along with a total fee of US$105. And we have to restrain ourselves from laughing after the customs officer takes such a long time checking each page and stamp in our passport, but still has to ask our nationality.

Thankful that all the paperwork is in order, we walk into the shanty village of Luperon. A little girl calls out 'hello, gringo'; these Spanish-speaking people are poor but very friendly. Small wooden houses line the streets intermingled with shops selling fruit and

Grand Turk Island

vegetables, and, unforgettably, a whole butchered beast hanging from the front of the shop. There's also a tiny supermarket selling rum, beer and cigars. Small motorbikes are everywhere; not only does every boy over the age of 12 have one but they also do service as taxis. It is not uncommon to see a whole family perched on a scooter (without helmets, of course).

Inland, everything is beautifully green and overall the island seems huge after all the much smaller ones we have visited over the last few weeks. We make our way down a road shared with cattle and hens and marvel at the mix of mostly poor and a few wealthy homes along the way. The border to Haiti is only 100 km to the west and with the immense poverty in that country many people cross the border illegally to make their home in the comparatively better-off DR, which causes the locals great concern. DR's population is nine

million (plus another one million 'illegals'), while Haiti has seven million.

We spend a day in the large city of Puerto Plata to stock up on provisions to take into Cuba, including a pile of non-perishables and luxury items to give away. Back in Luperon, Ian takes the opportunity to visit the dentist, a German, while we're here (I keep telling him that it's not a good idea to untie knots with your teeth, never mind using superglue to stick his tooth back in). While the dentist is drilling away the generator stops with a large bang ... no more drilling. The dentist asks an Australian in the next chair if he can help fix it and, still wearing his cape, he manages to get it operating again.

Medical treatment is always a big worry for us in these remote locations but thankfully we don't have too many problems. Ian is happy with the result of his visit (actually several visits) to the German dentist and

Arriving at Grand Turk Island

ends up getting four crowns in under a week for just over AU$1200. Dental work here is so cheap that people travel down from the USA, stay in an expensive resort and have new crowns fitted – all for less than the cost of getting one done at home.

The joy of having my benchtop covered in fresh tropical fruit again is wonderful; we especially relish the biggest and most flavourful pawpaw we've ever seen. Meeting a lot of cruisers has made this a very enjoyable place to stop. Plus the locals are among the nicest islanders we have met; maybe it's their Latino heritage coming through. Bahia de Luperon has a mixed reputation, but apart from the enclosed water not being suitable for swimming or desalinating, it has much to offer.

Preparing to depart for the Turks and Caicos Islands 85 nautical miles to the north we have our first-ever run-in with the authorities. After all our documents have been stamped, we are denied departure by the Commandant as he believes the weather is not suitable for a safe passage. It is only blowing 20 knots with a 2-metre swell from the east, but he stands firm. We think it's very odd because we're always so careful to know what's going on with the weather and we'd never put ourselves in danger. Our main concern is to ensure we arrive at the next port in daylight hours, and we strongly believe that the responsibility for deciding on when to leave should always lie with the skipper.

Anyway, on our return next day along with several other yachts requesting departure, we are finally granted permission to depart – and after handing over the mandatory $US20, we make our final preparations. What a lot of bureaucratic nonsense; we'll think twice about coming here again.

Leaving Providenciales

Providenciales, Turks and Caicos Islands

With only a day to spare to rendezvous with Mike and Di Quaife from Sydney in Grand Turk, we head off on an overnight sail under full moon. It's a fast and comfortable trip and we arrive at 5 am. However, it's now very dark as the full moon has disappeared behind a cloud and just as we arrive the autopilot goes down and the lighthouse is not operative. Edging ever so slowly towards the beach, we anchor, then sleep until daybreak.

Big Sand Cay, the southernmost of the Turks group of islands, is uninhabited and memorable for its white cliffs, a blown-over lighthouse and its stunning clear water.

This low-lying sand island set in very deep water (around 4000 metres) appears out of nowhere so it's little wonder that so many mariners do not see it until it is too late and they become grounded.

Pulling in beside us is *Why Not*, a lagoon catamaran which we passed during the night. On board is Terry Bufton – a stroke of luck because Terry is an aeronautical engineer and he manages to fix our autopilot hydraulics. Now retired, Terry spends much of his time helping to deliver yachts.

We have actually deviated off our planned route of sailing west to Cuba and the West Caribbean countries of Mexico, Belize and Guatemala to visit the Turks and Caicos Islands. Although they don't belong to the Bahamas or the Caribbean islands, the Turks and Caicos are nonetheless similar to the Bahamian islands (only 40 nautical miles away) with their low-lying sand cays and large areas of shallow reefs. A separate British Crown Colony since 1973, the islands have suffered from corruption issues including the disappearance of £5 million received from Britain to help fix the damage

Approaching Amanyara Resort, Providenciales Island

caused by hurricanes Ike and Hanna in September 2008. We see the evidence on Grand Turk with our own eyes: sheets of corrugated iron lying about while many houses remain roofless and the customs office in darkness because not all electricity has been restored.

Grand Turk claims to be the landing spot for Columbus on his voyage of discovery in 1492 (although this claim is also made by two Bahamian islands just west of here). Another claim to fame is that astronaut John Glenn came here after his famous space flight in 1962.

Although around two-thirds of the population live on Providenciales (known as Provo), the capital of Cockburn Town is actually on Grand Turk, which is inhabited by only a few hundred people. All the islands in the group rely heavily on tourism – the limited freshwater resources make any other industry difficult to develop (private cisterns collect rainwater for drinking). The primary

natural resources are spiny lobster, conch and other shellfish.

On our way to South Caicos Mike reels in a dorado that seems to get bigger and bigger the closer we get to the island. It's interesting how we always hook them as we approach land; apparently this is because the currents push fish into this area, making it an ideal feeding ground for the bigger fish. We also note that more often than not we're successful with our fishing either just after sunrise or just before sunset.

Cockburn Harbour on South Caicos is the safest anchorage in the Turks and Caicos, but our main reason for stopping here is to visit the lobster factory – eight lobster tails on the barbecue tonight!

Over the next two days we plan to take our time crossing to the island of Providenciales, 50 nautical miles away over a unique expanse of waterway known as the

Caicos Bank. What makes it so special is that it's very shallow and the colour of the sea over the white sand is amazing. Fortunately it's well charted with various named routes to choose between depending on the draft of one's yacht. We decide on the 'Pearl Highway', which allows a draft to 2.2 metres but as we draw 2 metres, it's pretty scary stuff and could never be negotiated at night. The clarity and colour of the sea and the sky are fantastic; as far as the eye can see there is the aquamarine sea and the blue skies with some white clouds that are tinged with the sea's reflection. This is the perfect sail and the only thing we have to do is watch for bombies. It's possible to see them in the distance as long as the sun is behind us. Then we just steer around them, even if they turn out to be only the shadow of a cloud. Halfway across we decide to anchor overnight – the sandy bottom is only a few centimetres beneath us – and just enjoy being in the middle of the ocean with no sign of land; it's a not-to-be missed experience. More lobster tails on the barbecue (sorry, staple diet here), a glass or two of Moët et Chandon Champagne, a compulsory swim in the morning and then we move on; there is nothing else here. The lobster is the best we have tasted in the Caribbean, small, very sweet and tender.

Providenciales, the glamour resort island, is next, but suddenly all our electrics go down. Under engine we get into a marina and as fate would have it no electrician can come for a week. But Terry, who resuscitated our autopilot back in the Turks, is here and once again comes to our rescue. A simple fuse is all it takes.

The north coast of Provo is where all the glamour is to be found but can only be entered in good weather as one has to pass through a narrow entrance in the reef at high tide. The weather looks good enough to do it so we sail around to the other side of the island into Grace Bay and anchor off Turtle Cove Marina. As we make our way back to the yacht after enjoying dinner ashore, we are approached by a dolphin that puts his nose up on the dinghy as if to say 'hello'. I recognise him instantly as JoJo, the famous wild dolphin I've been reading about. He loves to swim with people, but you can't touch him as he is known to bite. As it's a very large bay he lives in, and because he is quite old now, it's special when he comes to visit. The locals are thrilled to hear we've had this experience as he's not been seen for some time.

Amanyara Resort, Providenciales Island

Nikki Beach Bar and Resort, Providenciales Island

Lounging around a resort sounds like a nice change, so we take ourselves to Nikki Beach Bar and Resort for brunch to farewell Mike and Di. The pool and beach are equipped with white squabs and cabanas, turquoise towels to match the sea, a sunken bar and the obligatory palm trees. There's also a new marina to complete the setting with a number of 200-ft private yachts berthed there.

Enough lounging though, now it's time to prepare for our passage to the south side of Cuba.

Sapodilla Bay, Provo, Turks and Caicos Islands

From the north side of Provo we gently sail out of Grace Bay through Sellars Cut in the reef. En route around the western end of Provo, the luxurious Amanyara Resort takes our attention, so we anchor and go ashore for a look. It features Balinese-style thatched roof villas and is indeed very beautiful, but as our two cocktails come to $US50 we decided to make it a quick visit.

The bay where we're anchored is exposed to the north but as it's flat calm we decide to stay the night. The water is so transparent it is an ideal time for Ian to clean off the bottom and propeller. This year we painted the prop with Prop Speed but it seems to have had the opposite effect to its claims; it is absolutely covered in barnacles that really slow us down. The antifouling Micron 66 has also attracted a few patches of barnacles; this is unusual considering the seawater hasn't been as warm as normal.

On the south side of Provo at Sapodilla Bay we spend our days changing oil and the evenings being very social with all the cruising yachts passing through. There's nothing like a mix of Americans, Brits and Aussies all

Time to lie in the sun, Providenciales Island

discussing politics, arguing about which country has caused all the current financial problems.

After finding a fuel leak on the generator, we move to the Annex, a half-finished marina in Cooper Jack Bight, the entrance to a 2.5-mile canal system. It provides great shelter in the strong winds and has the advantage of no fees. Southside Marina is the next bay to the east, and as we are too deep to go in there Simon and Charlyn, who manage this very small, friendly and social marina, are very helpful in getting the problem fixed. Simon runs a cruisers' net daily on VHF radio on channel 18 to keep all cruisers up to date with weather and happenings. Tonight we enjoy a barbecue covered in local fresh lobster, in fact enough to feed over 20 of us – nothing like it!

Wind, lots of it. The locals like to tell us this is unusual, but we are only too happy not to be going north to the Bahamas. The north wind is persistent and can delay cruisers for up to two weeks in a bay.

Our last day here in the Turks and Caicos and what could be better than a day at Da Conch Shack and bar. I have finally given in to eating conch: conch fritters and cracked conch straight from the sea – delicious. This place is the last of the original beach bars here and is run by Jamaicans, lots of fun people. We will miss those big white smiles in the future whenever the word 'cricket' is mentioned.

Tomorrow we sail for Cuba, 245 nautical miles south to Santiago de Cuba on the south side. The weather looks perfect with 15 to 20 knots from just aft of the port beam and following seas.

Geoff and Pip Lavis from Sydney will join us for three weeks and we are very much looking forward to sharing the Cuban experience.

Recipes

Throughout the Caribbean mouth-watering tropical fruits can be found in abundance, especially at the local markets that offer a 'fruit salad' of mangos, passionfruit, bananas, pineapples, papayas and guava.

On board I'm never without the following:

🕶 The versatile and plentiful lime (preferably the large, juicy and slightly sweeter *Citrus* x *latifolia*), which can be used so many ways including in cocktails, marinating fish and even as a health remedy. They're also a great flavour booster; instead of salt try a squeeze of lime to enhance a meal.

🕶 The delicious pineapples grown throughout the Caribbean and which are readily available at any time of year (Christopher Columbus introduced the 'pine of the Indies' into Europe where it was used as a centrepiece on the dining table). I love to have them around because their acid content helps break down protein in the body making them an important part of our diet. When choosing a pineapple, pull out one of its leaves and if it comes easily you know the fruit is ripe and ready for eating.

🕶 The herbs and spices that, of course, enhance many different kinds of food but especially Creole cooking. The aromas of the different spices sold at local markets always draw me in, along with the freshness of the bundled spring onions, thyme and parsley that are grown locally.

🕶 Fresh fish – in my opinion nothing can match the taste of fish straight from the sea (sometimes we cook and eat it before we even get into port!). Cuban waters are especially full of sea life and we'll never get sick of the local lobsters and prawns.

Prawn Curry Roti

Filling for 4 wraps
500 g peeled and cooked prawns, shells reserved
lime juice
1 cup water
oil for frying
2 large onions
6 cloves garlic, peeled and crushed
3 tsp curry powder
5 large potatoes, peeled and diced
½ tsp chilli

4 roti wraps (thin Lebanese-style bread)

Sprinkle prawns with lime juice. Cook prawn shells in water for 20 minutes to make stock.

Heat a little oil in a frying pan and gently fry onions. Add garlic and curry powder, then potatoes and chilli. Pour stock into pan and cook for 30 minutes. Five minutes before end of cooking time, add prawns.

The mixture should be quite thick. Let cool, then wrap mixture in warmed rotis.

Cod Fritters

2 fillets salted codfish
milk
flour
2 eggs
1 clove garlic, peeled and crushed
1 tsp thyme leaves
2 spring onions, sliced
½ tsp crushed chilli

Soak salted codfish in milk for a few hours to remove saltiness, and remove flesh from bones. Mix together flour and enough milk to form a soft dough.

Mix in eggs, garlic, thyme, spring onions and chilli. Make fritters into small balls and deep fry.

Serve as a starter with cocktails.

Note: Prawns, lobster or crab can also be used in this recipe.

Tomato Fish Soup

1 cup water
fish bones and head
1 small onion
3 cloves garlic, crushed
2 cubes vegetable stock
2 Tbsp tomato purée
herbs as available
chilli to taste

cream and parsley for garnish

Put water, fish bones, onion, garlic, vegetable stock, tomato purée, herbs and chilli to taste in pot and boil together for 20 minutes, then strain.
Serve with fresh cream and parsley.

Island-spiced Mahi Mahi with Mango Curry

flour
mahi mahi steaks
olive oil for frying

3 tsp Colombo curry powder
2 tsp grated fresh ginger
1 tsp chilli
2 tsp chopped lemongrass
1 capsicum, diced
1 ripe mango, cubed
3 Tbsp rum
4 Tbsp coconut milk

Flour fish steaks. Heat oil in frying pan and cook fish.

In another pan, heat more olive oil and cook curry powder for 1 minute. Stir in ginger, chilli, lemongrass and capsicum. Cook for 1 minute and let cool.

Add mango, rum and coconut milk. Cook for 2 minutes or enough just to heat through.

Serve with sliced fresh pineapple and greens.

Jerk Chicken

4 chicken pieces

Marinade
2 Tbsp crushed pimento peppers or 2 Tbsp allspice
4 cloves garlic, peeled and crushed
¼ cup brown sugar
1 bunch thyme, leaves only
1 tsp chilli
2 spring onions, finely sliced
½ tsp cinnamon
½ tsp nutmeg
salt
3 Tbsp soy sauce

Mix marinade and coat the chicken pieces in this for at least 2 hours or overnight.
   Barbecue or grill meat, but take care not to burn it. Pour a little beer or water over to prevent burning.

Caribbean Guacamole

2 firm avocados, chopped
2 tsp cumin powder or Colombo curry powder
juice of 1 lime or 2 lemons
1 Tbsp chopped spring onion or coriander
½ tsp chilli
2 cloves garlic, peeled and crushed

Blend all ingredients together with a fork (do not mash).

Chicken Satay on Skewers

chicken pieces

Marinade
1 onion, peeled and finely sliced
1 clove garlic, peeled and crushed
2 Tbsp soy sauce
½ tsp chilli
1 tsp ground coriander
2 tsp brown sugar
1 Tbsp lime juice
1 Tbsp olive oil

Mix marinade and coat the chicken pieces in this for at least 2 hours or overnight.
   Skewer chicken pieces on damp wooden skewers. Grill or barbecue until chicken is cooked through.

Sauce
1¼ cups coconut milk
4 Tbsp crunchy peanut butter
1 Tbsp Thai fish sauce
salt and pepper

Combine ingredients and cook for 3 minutes. Serve over cooked chicken skewers.

Cabbage Coleslaw with Pineapple and Peanuts

½ cabbage, thinly sliced
½ fresh pineapple, cut into small pieces
½ cup peanuts
½ cup raisins
½ cup mayonnaise or sour cream
2 Tbsp vinegar
2 tsp honey

Mix first 4 ingredients together. Combine mayonnaise or sour cream, vinegar and honey and mix into salad.

Banana Leaf-wrapped Fish with Coconut and Coriander Sauce

½ onion, peeled and very finely chopped
1 bunch fresh coriander, chopped
1 cup white wine
150 ml fish stock
½ cup coconut milk
2 Tbsp butter
4 fish fillets
salt and pepper to taste
extra butter for brushing
banana leaves
lime wedges

Put onion, coriander stems and white wine in a pot and cook until syrupy. Add fish stock and coconut milk. Reduce and strain. Whisk in butter and add chopped coriander leaves.

Season fish fillets, brush with butter and top with lime wedges. Wrap in banana leaf and cook in oven for 7 minutes.

Serve coated with sauce.

Steak with Green Peppercorn Sauce

This is an absolutely great sauce, very French Caribbean.

2 Tbsp green peppercorns crushed with
    some olive oil
2 Tbsp wholeseed mustard
1 Tbsp HP or barbecue sauce
2 Tbsp cream
3 Tbsp water
steak

Mix first 5 ingredients together but do not cook.

Cook steak as desired, dress with sauce and serve with mashed potato and greens.

Hot Potato Herb Salad

4 large potatoes, peeled, boiled until firm
    and drained
1 clove garlic, peeled and finely chopped
½ red capsicum, diced
olive oil for frying
4 spring onions, sliced
fresh parsley
fresh thyme
1 Tbsp olive oil
2 Tbsp cider vinegar

Fry potatoes, garlic and capsicum in a little olive oil.
    Stir in spring onions, parsley and thyme when ready
to serve. Pour on second measure of olive oil and cider
vinegar and combine.
    Note: Any leftovers can be stirred into a breakfast
omelette.

Raw Marinated Fish

500 g fresh fish (e.g. tuna, mahi mahi, sail fish or
    raw prawns)
2 tomatoes, peeled and diced
1 onion, peeled and chopped
juice of 2 limes
salt and pepper
½ can coconut cream (optional)
parsley
spring onion greens or chives, sliced

Cut fish into small cubes and soak in salt water for 1 hour.
    Fold tomatoes and onion into drained fish cubes. Add
lime juice. Season with salt and pepper and marinate for
1 hour.
    Just before serving, add coconut cream if using and
garnish with parsley and spring onion greens. (For a fresh
flavour omit the coconut cream.)

Colombo Curried Chicken on Caesar Salad with Pineapple

chicken fillets, thinly sliced
Colombo curry powder
brown sugar
butter for frying

Coat chicken fillets with curry powder and sprinkle with
brown sugar. Fry in butter until tender, then cut into
pieces.

Caesar Salad
crisp lettuce leaves
Parmesan cheese
spring onions, sliced
fresh coriander or basil

Aïoli
1 egg yolk
1 clove garlic, peeled and crushed
olive oil
juice of 1 lemon

Combine lettuce, Parmesan, spring onion and coriander
or basil. To make aïoli, combine egg yolk and crushed
garlic. Slowly whisk in olive oil and then add lemon juice.
Use to dress salad.
    Arrange on platter with the salad first, then chicken
pieces on top, then aïoli dressing. Accompany with fresh
pineapple or mango slices.

Lobster – again (top)
Avocados are plentiful everywhere (bottom)

Quick Duck Breast à l'Orange

If the duck breast fillet is large, it will feed 2 people.

1 duck breast fillet
oil for frying
½ cup white wine
½ cup water
2 heaped Tbsp good quality orange marmalade

Fry fillet of duck skin-side down in a little oil with lid on for 10 minutes. Turn to meat side occasionally. Pour in white wine and water. Add marmalade and let simmer for 10 minutes, then with lid off continue cooking until sauce thickens. Duck should still be a little rare.
Slice and serve covered with the sauce, green beans and potato gratin.

Marinated Fish with Spicy Herb Dressing

fish
salt
lime juice
garlic, peeled and crushed

Marinate fish in combined salt, lime juice and garlic.

Dressing
juice of 1 lime
2 spring onions, chopped
1 Tbsp chives
1 sprig thyme
2 cloves garlic, peeled and crushed
¼ tsp minced chilli
1 Tbsp chopped parsley
¼ cup cider vinegar
2 Tbsp olive oil
¼ cup boiling water

Mix first 9 ingredients together and just before serving add boiling water. Serve over grilled fish.

Mango Chutney

small piece of fresh ginger, grated
1 onion, peeled and chopped
3 Tbsp apple cider vinegar
3 Tbsp sugar
1 Tbsp Cajun spice
2 ripe mangos, chopped
freshly chopped mint for serving

Lightly pan-fry ginger and chopped onion. Add vinegar, sugar, Cajun spice and mango. Cook over low heat for 30 minutes. Stir in fresh chopped mint when serving.
   Serve with lobster or fish.

Fish with Creole Sauce

Per person
2 fillets fish
juice of 2 limes
½ tsp chilli
1 clove garlic, peeled and crushed
salt
oil for frying
2 tomatoes, peeled and diced
2 spring onions, chopped
1 tsp thyme leaves
extra clove garlic, peeled and crushed
juice of 1 extra lime

Marinate fish for 1 hour in combined lime juice, chilli, garlic and salt. Fry fish in hot oiled pan and remove to a warm place.
   Add tomatoes, spring onions, thyme leaves, garlic and lime juice to pan and warm through without cooking. Pour over fish to serve.

Caribbean Pineapple Colombo Curry Rice

olive oil for frying
4 spring onions, chopped
1 piece ginger, peeled and grated
½ tsp chilli
1 chopped red horn pepper or capsicum
2 Tbsp Colombo curry powder
1 cup cooked rice per person, drained
1 ripe fresh pineapple, cubed

Heat a little oil in a frying pan and fry spring onions, ginger, chilli, horn pepper or capsicum and Colombo curry powder. Add rice and chopped pineapple to warm through.
   Serve with lightly crumbed fish fillets and slices of fresh papaya or mango.

BBQ Whole Fish with Tamarind Sauce

whole fish, cleaned and gutted

Tamarind Sauce
oil for frying
1 clove garlic, peeled and chopped
small piece ginger, peeled and grated
½ tsp chilli
2 Tbsp brown sugar
½ cup fish sauce
4 Tbsp tamarind sauce
juice of 2 limes
chopped basil, coriander or spring onions to garnish

Cut deep slashes in fish. Wrap in foil and barbecue.
   In a frying pan cook garlic and ginger in a little oil. Add chilli (be careful not to burn it), brown sugar, fish sauce, tamarind sauce and lime juice. Cook to thicken.
   Serve over barbecued fish and garnish with chopped basil, coriander or spring onions.

Coconut Shrimp Fritters

1 cup flour
2 eggs, lightly beaten
½ cup grated fresh coconut
juice of 1 lime
dash Tabasco sauce
1 tsp baking powder
1 clove garlic, peeled and crushed
salt
1 tsp ground coriander
1 small onion, peeled and finely chopped
500 g cooked shrimps, peeled and chopped
oil for frying

Mix together flour, eggs, grated coconut and lime juice to form a soft dough. Fold in remaining ingredients and form mixture into small balls. Deep-fry for a few minutes. Serve with cocktail sauce made by mixing together the ingredients listed below.

Cocktail Sauce
2 Tbsp tomato sauce
juice of 2 limes
2 Tbsp mayonnaise
1 tsp chilli

Tasty market food, Guatemala

Lime Cream Sauce with Baked Fish

Lime Cream Sauce
1 onion, peeled and chopped
oil for frying
½ cup white wine
½ cup fish stock
1 Tbsp thyme
zest and juice of 2 limes
¼ cup cream
salt and white pepper

fish

Sauté onion in oil in a frying pan. Add wine, fish stock, thyme and lime zest and juice. Cook until reduced and thickened. Add cream and season to taste.
  Wrap fish topped with lime slices and thyme in foil and bake for 20 minutes in a hot oven.
  Serve fish coated with sauce.

Dorado Fish in Coriander Green Curry

Make your own Green Curry Paste according to the following recipe or use ½ jar prepared Goya green curry (available in the Caribbean).

Green Curry Sauce
1 bunch fresh coriander
½ tsp chilli
1 tsp cumin powder
1 tsp coriander powder
1 clove garlic, peeled and crushed
1 small piece ginger, peeled and grated
1 small spring onion, sliced
1 green horn pepper or 1 green capsicum

½ can coconut milk
1 Tbsp brown sugar or palm sugar
1 Tbsp fish sauce
juice of 2 limes

fish

Blend together first 8 ingredients and cook over low heat for a few minutes. Add remaining ingredients and mix in. Fry or poach fish fillet in curry sauce.

Quick Thousand Island Dressing

⅓ cup tomato juice
juice of 2 limes
⅓ cup mayonnaise
½ tsp puréed chilli

Mix all ingredients together. Serve with fresh cooked prawns.

Herbed Stuffed Pork and Pineapple

1 pork leg, deboned but leave skin on for crackling

Stuffing
1 cup fresh breadcrumbs
2 eggs
1 cup chopped pineapple
½ cup pine nuts
3 Tbsp fresh herbs (thyme, rosemary, etc)
1 onion, peeled and chopped
½ tsp chilli

salt
oil
rosemary sprigs
½ cup water
2 stock cubes
4 cloves garlic
2 lemons, halved

Score the pork skin with a sharp knife. Mix together stuffing ingredients, place stuffing inside pork and tie with string. Salt and oil skin.

Line baking pan with sprigs of rosemary and place meat on top. Add water, stock cubes, garlic and lemon halves.

Bake for 3 hours in medium oven. Squeeze lemon halves and cooked garlic pulp into juices in pan, mix well and sieve for gravy.

Serve with hot or cold fresh sliced pineapple.

Grilled Pineapple Topped with Prawns

3 jumbo raw prawns per person
1 pineapple
brown sugar
oil or butter for frying

Marinade
1 Tbsp Colombo curry powder
2 small onions, peeled and chopped
3 cloves garlic, peeled and crushed
½ tsp zest of lemon or lime

Mix marinade ingredients together and marinate green prawns in this.

Peel and cut pineapple into ½ inch thick rounds, remove core and coat in brown sugar. Fry pineapple in a little oil or butter until golden and cook prawns lightly in marinade.

Serve prawns on top of pineapple with a dollop of aioli. Plate up with steamed rice and green beans.

Pickled Ginger

1 cup honey
1 cup sugar
½ cup cider vinegar
fresh ginger, peeled and thinly sliced

In a pan bring to the boil honey, sugar and cider vinegar. Add ginger slices and cook for 30 minutes, then let cool. Place in jars and refrigerate.

Leftover syrup can be used for making sauces.

Caribbean Island Salsa with Lobster and Garlic Sweet Potato

3 sweet potatoes, peeled and
    cut into bite-sized pieces
olive oil for frying
3 cloves garlic, peeled and chopped

Easy Asian-style Sauce
¼ cup sweet chilli sauce
1 Tbsp chopped pickled ginger or
    grated fresh ginger
juice of 2 limes
1 Tbsp fish sauce
1 tsp honey or to taste
mango, papaya, pineapple, honeydew melon,
    watermelon (whatever you have), chopped
1 Spanish onion, peeled and chopped
1 red capsicum, chopped
mint or coriander, chopped

green (uncooked) lobster meat
lightly beaten egg
½ cup fine breadcrumbs

Boil sweet potatoes until just firm and drain. Heat olive oil in frying pan and fry sweet potatoes until browned. In the last few minutes add garlic.

Combine sauce ingredients. Gently stir sauce through fruit, onion and capsicum and fold in mint or coriander.

Coat green lobster meat in egg and fine breadcrumbs and lightly fry in a little oil.

To serve, place potatoes on a plate, then top with crumbed lobster and cover with salsa.

Second Season
Cuba–Guatemala

Cathedral, Parques
Cespedes,
Santiago de Cuba

Market,
Santiago de Cuba

138

One of many pre-revolution 1950s American cars in Santiago de Cuba

Santiago de Cuba, Cuba

Our sail to the eastern tip of Cuba in fresh winds from the Turks is exciting. Once in the lee of the island on the south side we sail 100 nautical miles west to Santiago de Cuba. Halfway we are confronted by the might of the US military in the form of a patrol boat armed with machine guns and a cannon pointing directly at us. Passing Guantanamo Bay, the United States Naval Base, we wish to take a closer look but are immediately informed via VHF radio that we are close to US Territory (I seem to recall Rudd and Obama are meeting about now – surely we're all on the same side?) and ordered to identify ourselves. It actually takes the operator six attempts to obtain all the information he claims to need.

The ocean boundary is 3 nautical miles offshore and extends along the shore for over 8 nautical miles. The patrol boat stays between us and the shore for over an hour and I have to say it is a bit nerve-racking watching the 20-year-old gunner with his finger on the trigger. I hope a large wave doesn't cause his finger to slip!

Free at last, we sail on to a very different port of entry: Santiago de Cuba. We are greeted by the sight of the historic Castillo de San Pedro del Morro fort built by the Spanish in 1633 on the steep headland. We don't know it but our lesson in communism is about to begin.

Our Cruising Guide has not been revised for 10 years and we are expecting a filthy harbour, a rickety wharf, a line-up of officials wanting gifts and – if we are lucky – some other cruisers for company. This is definitely not the case. From the moment we enter the fiord-like harbour, there's a wow factor! The water is clean; there's a stunning backdrop of mountains; palm trees everywhere and we spot some locals at the beach. What's more, the marina is full of cruising yachts, 10 of them. What we also notice

Ian's Cruising Notes
MEDICAL MATTERS

We carry a comprehensive medical kit with all the standard medications, ointments, bandages and plasters plus injections for local anaesthetic (and chronic seasickness), needle and thread for stitches, and temporary tooth fillings. While antibiotics are normally easy to obtain from most pharmacies, we carry reserves.

In case of an emergency our satellite phone is programmed with the numbers for two doctors who are both well known to us; one in the northern hemisphere and one in the southern.

though is the lack of paint and general maintenance everywhere we look. It's as if time has stood still for 50+ years. But the beauty of the place and the friendly people all making the most of what they have make up for the shabbiness.

Today is the 50th anniversary of the revolution and a holiday. Once we finish our dealings with the pleasant uniformed military officials (I lose count of the number), including a doctor to make sure we are not carrying any diseases, and a sniffer dog, we join a spontaneous 50th party ashore with a pig on the spit and soon make a whole new set of friends.

It's our first 24 hours in Cuba, and Ian feels like he has died and gone to heaven surrounded as we are by wonderful music, mojitos and so many friendly Spanish-speaking people. As for me, it is an enlightening experience. I'm wide-eyed at all the fantastic images everywhere we look.

Irish Nick on *Val* is single-handedly sailing his way around the world and wants us to join him early the next morning to visit the farmers' market in the centre of the city 10 kilometres away. The main square, Parque Cespedes, is just as we expect: Spanish architecture, some crumbling and some being restored; colourful 1950s American cars and an old woman smoking a cigar.

Cuba uses two currencies, which causes us some confusion to begin with. Tourists use Cuban convertible currency (CUC) and the locals use national pesos. This situation has come about as a result of the communist economy in combination with US sanctions and some other factors. What it means on a day-to-day basis is that the locals have to use the national peso to buy essential foodstuffs, but 'dollar shops', which sell just about everything else, only accept the tourist CUC. To be able to do the kind of shopping we want, we need both currencies.

The farmers' market is a rustic affair and everything is really cheap (and can only be bought with local pesos). Farmers have only recently been able to sell their produce on the open market and although limited, it's seasonal and very fresh. As for fresh meat, there's pork, and pork and pork. All that pig is going to test my creative skills, but at least we will end up with healthy hearts.

Next, it's time for coffee at the 1920s Casa Grande Hotel with its open veranda and art deco lights overlooking the square. Salsa music fills the air, old men on benches strum guitars, and a number of Africans are singing and dancing to their own music. There's any number of small café/bar theatres that offer free shows during the day where we watch the locals do their thing. One such place is Casa de la Trova and we spend many hours listening to everything around us over lunch in the Spanish-style open-air courtyard. This is the home of Cuban music and many famous bands including the Buena Vista Social Club whose 70+-year-old performers toured the world for some years after they were discovered. We learn that Cuba invented the mojito and we enjoy many of these delicious cocktails (a rum and coke in this part of the world equates to a bottle of rum **and** a bottle of coke – all for AU$5!).

We need to get ourselves back to the yacht to freshen up. Our ride back to the marina is in a sky-blue 1948 Buick and as I sink back into the old blue leather seats the petrol engine roars into life and romantic salsa music fills the car. I can barely see out the window from the depths of the seat, but it's so much fun – straight out of the movie *Grease*. The cute driver really loves his car and we arrange for him to come back to pick us up when we're ready.

Colourful ladies of the night, passionate salsa dancing, hustlers teaching the girls how to move, and slurping on long mojitos as the bands do their thing on stage; we don't

There's any number of small café/bar theatres that offer free shows during the day where we watch the locals do their thing. One such place is Casa de la Trova.

want the night to end. At 2 am there are not a lot of cars around, so we take our life in our hands and get a ride in a 1970s Russian Lada, a beat-up heap. We coast down hills to save fuel and on arrival at the marina the car loses its exhaust pipe.

The next two days are spent at the marina just enjoying the weather and generally mucking about. We have no choice but to moor here as the local rules do not allow us to anchor out so we cannot use the dinghy to explore. But we do however have power, water and Havana Club rum at only US$4.00 a bottle.

Now it's time to get out and about and try to see what the authorities don't want the tourists to see! We hire a driver for the morning and for our first stop we check out the Montecristo Cigar factory, rated number two in the world behind another Cuban brand, Cohiba. The factory has 250 employees who produce 20,000 hand-made cigars (*totalmente a mano*) a day. Unfortunately we are not permitted to take any photographs of the hard-working locals who earn about US$30 a month.

The back streets show the other side of Cuba. Dirt roads recently dug up in an effort to repair water pipes that have not been touched since before the revolution in 1959 and bland Soviet Union-built tenements that are free to all Cubans. There are even people using horse and cart-style transport due to lack of fuel. What does come as a surprise to us is that most people are well dressed. It's just the local infrastructure that is in such bad shape and I hate to think what will happen if this state of affairs continues for much longer.

The only advertising we see are images on large billboards of the founding revolutionaries, including Fidel Castro and Che Guevara promoting the 50th anniversary of their success on 1 January 1959. Cuba has been a communist country ever since and the signs of this failed dream are everywhere. Castro overthrew a corrupt capitalist government that had been sponsored by the USA since 1899. Before that time it had been controlled by Spain since the arrival of Columbus in 1492. In 1868 Spanish landowners rebelled against control by Spain and this was followed by another rebellion in 1895 led by Jose Marti, which resulted in the US involvement.

On a happier note the Santiago de Cuba musical festival has just started, an event that will make our stay very special.

PS: Communications in Cuba are not easy. We can't use our mobile, and email (on old computers) is only available at hotels, which involves having to produce our passports every time.

Santiago de Cuba–Cienfuegos

Geoff and Pip Lavis have now joined us for the 350-nautical-mile sail west along the south coast of Cuba to Cienfuegos and Cayo Largo, passing the Sierra Maestra Mountains and on through the many cays of the Archipielago de los Jardines de la Reina (Queen's Gardens).

Provisioning has been an interesting exercise. Free eggs are allocated at 10 per person per month; somehow we manage to acquire someone else's quota as well as getting some more on the black market. We don't feel guilty about this; everyone here is eager to get some Cuban convertible currency. A taxi driver uses his coupons to get some bread for us, but there is just one style of loaf available. Cakes we wouldn't even consider buying, even though they are free, but again just one kind – a sponge coated with mock cream – is available. There's only seasonal fruit and vegetables but they're cheap and easy to buy – but only with local pesos.

As I said earlier, the two currencies are confusing and the situation has created a class difference; not only for tourists but also for the locals. Only those who have managed to acquire CUCs may shop at the 'dollar shops'. A lot of educated people have now turned to the tourist industry as it is a way of acquiring the more valuable currency.

We enjoy our two-week stay at the marina with its pleasant staff and more services than we expected. Cruisers come and go ... some to Jamaica, others to the Dominican Republic or some heading west like us. We experience some acid rain from a nearby refinery that leaves small yellow spots on the deck. (Memo to world leaders: clean-up should start here?)

We continue our sightseeing and particularly enjoy visiting Moncada Barracks, the site of Fidel Castro's first attack against the ruling and corrupt Batista government on 26 July 1953. You can still see the bullet holes on the outside of the building, while inside the history of the uprising is shown in detail.

The local cemetery, Santa Ifigenia, is another site worth visiting as here rest the martyrs from the many uprisings since 1868 when the cemetery was established. Every half hour there is a changing of the goose-stepping honour guard for the tomb of Jose Marti (1853–95), a national hero revered by all. The Bacardi Rum family are also here plus original Buena Vista Social Club band member Comay Segundo, who died in 2003.

While in Santiago we meet Jesus, the skipper of a charter catamaran, and before we leave he recommends a number of wonderfully unspoilt cays and anchorages for us to visit.

There's not a lot of wind for our departure, due to the protection of the mountain range (the highest mountain in the range is 1973 metres), but it's a perfect day for fishing, whales and dolphins. Many of the barracuda we catch are thrown back but we keep the four tuna that are hooked two at a time on separate lines.

Pilon, a tiny sugar town 175 km west from Santiago de Cuba, is a night stop and next day it's on to Cabo Cruz, the southernmost part of Cuba, where we anchor behind a breaking reef with a lighthouse. It's a superb swimming bay and we enjoy a beautiful sunset while watching the fishermen row out to get lobster. We feel really secure so that when we reach for our beach towels the next morning and find them missing along with Ian's old but treasured Sperry sandals, we're quite shattered. For the first time in our seven years of cruising we experience that horrible feeling of someone being on board while we sleep. It's not worth reporting; it's only petty theft and at least they didn't take any of the more valuable things such as our fishing rod. But it still leaves us with an uneasy feeling. We've felt really safe here; safer than anywhere else we've ever been so this intrusion is quite a surprise, but fortunately an isolated experience.

Even though there's little wind, the boys hoist the spinnaker but we end up mostly motoring, which is quite relaxing, to Jardines de la Reina (Queen's Gardens), a chain of hundreds of small uninhabited white sand cays covered in mangroves. The only people out here are the fishermen and us. During the next nine days we day-hop to different cays, entering shallow bays surrounded by coral and in this time we see only three other yachts.

We're here to experience one of our favourite culinary delights and we're not disappointed. Geoff and Ian go off in the dinghy and approach a fishing station inside a mangrove inlet. There they come across old rusty ferro-cement fishing boats (some floating and others washed ashore), lobster cages piled high and about 10 men working in appalling conditions. At first they don't appear to have any lobsters, but when Ian pulls out a bottle of rum and three cans of coke seven big lobsters appear.

Dinner that night is lobster cooked on the barbecue and served with garlic butter.

Our next anchorage, Cayo Anclitas, is a superb horseshoe bay and we share it with one other yacht. Ashore, it's perfect with live conch shells lining the water's edge but we do notice some strange trail marks that lead from the water up to the bushes. Assuming they're bike tracks or maybe caused by the roll of an anchor chain, we ignore them and set off to explore and pick up a few shells, but too many bugs in the evening heat send us back to the yacht. Not long after we get back we are visited by a fisherman and we barter two bottles of rum for 10 lobsters, which with a big smile he then sets out to catch. Soon after the people on the other yacht come over to ask if we've seen the crocodiles on the beach. Crocodiles? The four of us sit with our mouths hanging open, absolutely stunned.

After half an hour the fisherman returns with 23 lobsters! Lobster omelette for breakfast, cold lobster with Thousand Island dressing for lunch and lobster green curry for dinner. Out of the last eight consecutive meals, seven include lobster. So much for healthy hearts.

We sail on to where the prawn fishing fleet is based in Cayo Cuervo. An approach to some fishermen on one of the big ships doesn't get Ian anywhere until the rum comes out, at which point he's invited on board. Returning with 6 kg of green prawns we turn them into five delicious meals. Rum to date has been a very useful currency, but we may just enjoy a pork chop tonight.

On arriving at Cayos Machos de Fuera, one of the many places recommended by Jesus, the catamaran skipper in Santiago, we find a cay that's a natural habitat for endangered mammals. Ashore a caretaker takes us on an amazing circumnavigation of the island that takes us in and out of the mangroves. We sight birds, iguanas and *jutia* (tree rats the size of cats) all living with no fear of humans. Fortunately, there are no crocodiles. A lot of animals became endangered, especially the tree rat, as so many of them were eaten by Cubans when food was scarce during Castro's 'special period of austerity' after the fall of the Soviet Union in 1991.

After nine days of near isolation, we look forward to returning to civilisation. A 20-knot northeasterly wind is perfect for the 55-nautical-mile sail along the mountainous coast to the classic city of Cienfuegos. On our arrival we enter a narrow entrance and sail across the big enclosed bay to the marina.

Cienfuegos—Cayo Largo

Arriving in Marina Jagua on Punta Gorda, we admire the dilapidated but stately old buildings that were the waterfront 'weekenders' which once belonged to the rich in the pre-revolution era. The city was settled by French immigrants from Bordeaux and Louisiana, led by Don Louis D'Clouet in 1819, resulting in a wonderful French style of architecture. The town centre is only 10 minutes away from the marina and we get there via horse and cart, clip-clopping our way down the wide tree-lined avenue passing classic cars and more heritage housing. I find this city particularly memorable because of the enormous contrast between its beautiful buildings and the way the inhabitants live in a time warp.

It's so very different to Santiago de Cuba that we wonder if we are still in Cuba. But there are reminders: shops depleted of goods and people queuing for bread and their quota of eggs. Finding a rundown 1950s-style ice-cream parlour, we prepare to join the locals queuing down the street, but tourists take priority and don't have to wait. I guess we are at least paying, but there are only three flavours on offer. Our ice-creams consist of one scoop taken from a large old bowl using an ancient battered and bent aluminium spoon.

Once again our trip to the market for fresh produce is frustrating because of limited supplies but Pip and Geoff enjoy the banter. Pip spies an old woman discreetly holding just one egg. The woman calls her over and shows her, hidden under a shelf, a bag full. The ever-present flies are all over the fresh meat on sale, but Pip reassures Geoff that they are only houseflies. Ian negotiates to buy a leg of pork and is somewhat ripped off, but when I cook it the next day the smell of it makes it all worthwhile.

Cienfuegos was hit badly by Hurricane Dennis in 2005, but UNESCO came to the rescue with funds to help with the restoration of this World Heritage site. Although it's a beautiful city, for us Santiago de Cuba is more satisfying with its music, history, hustle and bustle.

From here we sail out to the next group of islands, Archipielago de los Canarreos and Pip and Geoff's final destination, Cayo Largo. As we leave, we pass the unfinished Soviet nuclear power station; unfinished thank goodness because it's positioned right on the water's edge. With the wind astern of us, the gennaker is set for the 45-nautical-mile sail to Cayo Guano del Este but between us and this destination is a naval exclusion zone set by Castro after the disastrous Bay of Pigs invasion by Cuban exiles and sponsored by the USA in 1960. We take our chances and cross safely through the zone.

Arriving at the deserted island, we anchor for the night under an amazing lighthouse that looks like a rocket ship. It's a memorable night; with little protection, the wind picks up and waves toss us about, testing our anchor. As long as I can see that lighthouse out of my starboard porthole I'm able to get some sleep but we all have a bad night. Geoff reports that at about 2 am the lighthouse lost its power for a while when the generator went down. All a bit scary, so at first light we leave for Cayo Largo, Cuba's famous resort island.

Many people will recall the song 'Kokomo' by the Beach Boys, which refers to Cayo Largo. It is up there with other beautiful spots in the Caribbean. As we enter the reef, the fabulous-looking and renowned beach of Playa Sirena welcomes us. We anchor off the beach and enjoy the rest of the day ashore. We arrange a short tour of some of the more famous resorts and although it's an interesting experience we note they are now pretty run down, yet are still packed with tourists, many of whom

Many people will recall the song 'Kokomo' by the Beach Boys, which refers to Cayo Largo. It is up there with other beautiful spots in the Caribbean.

We love Cuba, despite its problems including the
confusing currency, and we highly recommend
all cruisers and others to visit.

are French Canadians or from Spanish-speaking countries. After our tour we can't wait to get back on board and head out into the waters of the bay to enjoy some of the best mojitos and the feeling of sand under our feet again.

It's a special time cruising through the Cuban islands with Pip and Geoff, drinking too much rum and filling up on fresh seafood at every opportunity. But here at Cayo Largo, as in every single port we have called at, we are thoroughly checked, searched and asked for more paperwork. Cayo Largo is our last port of call and although the officials are very courteous, their presence is a bit of an intrusion, especially when they bring a smelly sniffer dog on board as we check out (we assume this is because we might have some locals hidden away).

We love Cuba, despite its problems including the confusing currency, and we highly recommend all cruisers and others to visit, especially before it opens up. Our hope for their future, which reflects the desire of all the locals we spoke to, is that the rush to capitalism will be controlled and will follow a European model rather than the excesses of the USA.

Cubans are looking for change in the near future. They believed in the revolution that brought them equality, and they have made the most of it living happily with what was available for a long time now (nothing is wasted – even our discarded empty plastic bottles are pounced on as treasure as we left). But the standard of living for the majority is not good, despite free housing, food, education, health and a guaranteed albeit very low wage. But it is not enough.

We find Cubans to be very welcoming and while we are here we become part of the underground black market for fuel, produce and wine. But we are never particularly comfortable about this. On the islands it becomes especially difficult for us to buy fresh food and on several occasions I find myself hiding in the guard's sentry box and once even in a toilet, all to avoid the ever-present official eyes. It's the same for fuel – in order to buy it, Ian has to secretly collect it in the dinghy, making sure the tanks are covered by a tarpaulin. This system leaves itself wide open to corruption and the hustlers in the main cities (often educated people trying to earn some CUC currency) wear us down trying to sell

us stuff and sometimes just begging. They are desperate for our money but we can't help everyone. When finally Americans can travel and sail to these shores it will greatly change things. Meanwhile, it has been a very special experience for us and one day we hope to return.

Due to the swine flu epidemic in Mexico, we have been advised not to sail there, not least because we may experience some difficulty entering other countries if we have visited the source of the flu. But it's not a problem, we just sail in a different direction – due south 145 nautical miles to the Cayman Islands, southwest to the Bay Islands of Honduras and then up the Rio Dulce of Guatemala. If things settle down in Mexico, we may try to visit the bordering country of Belize.

Cuba–Cayman–Honduras

Our 18-hour overnight sail to Grand Cayman Island from Cuba was heightened by the sight of the Southern Cross on the bow in the night sky. It's a great feeling to know we are now on the home run. Cayman was never on our radar, but it turns into a very pleasant stopover. Sitting in the middle of nowhere, this small flat island is surrounded by pristine waters that are the clearest we have seen anywhere. Buoys can be picked up free of charge (to protect the coral) and while we are here up to seven cruise ships at any one time tower behind us, including some that have been diverted from Mexico.

The day we arrive happens to coincide with the Batabano Carnival Parade, started in 1983 by the local Rotary club and featuring colourful costumes and loud reggae music. The normally religious locals have a lot of fun because it's the one time of year that they get to let their hair down and show a bit of skin. Cayman is full of ex-pats from every corner of the world, plus a mix of Caribbean colour from the other islands around here.

The Caymans are made up of three islands with Cayman as the capital. Discovered by Christopher Columbus in 1503 (how he stumbled on it is anyone's guess) they did not attract any great attention until they became a tax haven in the 1960s. Now with over 700 banks in permanent residence, it is also home to over 70 per cent of the world's hedge funds. At least we know the bankers are comfortable while they lose all our money. While locals don't pay any income or company tax, the tax on all consumer goods is very high to compensate.

Expecting Seven Mile Beach (it's actually only 4 miles) to be lined with high-rise apartment buildings, we are pleasantly surprised to find restrictions limit developments to just five storeys. The stylish resorts are few in number and in my opinion it's one of the most attractive Caribbean resort beaches we have visited. After the austerity of Cuba we treat ourselves to lunch at the Ritz Carlton poolside bar. Considering Grand Cayman was devastated by Hurricane Ivan in 2004, it has made an amazing recovery, particularly when you consider that no one was prepared given it had been 80 years since the last hurricane.

Along the way we've continued to make friends with fellow sailors, including Yaron whom we came across when we were in Cayo Largo. An ex-pat German, he's a doctor on Grand Cayman and often embarks on a quick sail on his small catamaran to Cayo Largo (135 nautical miles away) for a long weekend. We sail back to Grand Cayman together and he invites us for a barbecue lunch to his beachside house where we meet his wife and young family. It is nice to enjoy some home comforts again. Yaron and his wife love it here, so much so that they will never return home.

Swimming with stingrays, a popular tourist activity, is a must-do while we're here, but as the shallow sandbank where the stingrays congregate is not suitable for our yacht we join a group on *Red Sail*, a 60-ft catamaran that takes us out to the sandbank. My nerves are a bit strung out after taking my first step that sees me standing on a ray's razor tail. It quickly slides away but there are just so many of these 1-metre-wide creatures swimming in and out between our legs. One appears to take a fancy to me while I'm snorkelling around and comes up under me, as if to take me for a ride. I miss my beat, gulp in seawater and can't get away fast enough. It's actually an awesome experience as they are quite harmless; in fact they just seemed to want a cuddle.

Our last big sail of the season is a two-day 350-nautical-mile passage to the Bay Islands on the north coast of Honduras. The weather window is excellent with 15 knots predicted from the east. Weaving our way out between the cruise ships, we set the gennaker and stays up for the next 24 hours – nice. Then it starts to blow and under reefed

Georgetown, Grand Cayman

Stingrays, Grand Cayman

Poolside at Grand Cayman

sails we have a very fast run to the Bay Islands.

During the sail we take on two 'stowaways'. It's not the first time birds that have been lost at sea have landed on our yacht but they are generally so tired and dehydrated that they don't survive. It's no different this time and although I do everything I can these two beautiful goldfinches both die.

Wanting to arrive at our next landfall in daylight, we slow down. The island of Roatan is surrounded by a coral reef that quickly falls off to very deep water. We weave our way through the dog-leg channel, poorly marked with sticks taped with bands of faded red and green, into Roatan's French Cay Harbour as the full moon disappears and the sun rises. We finally end up in the sheltered harbour behind the reef. We later learn that it's normal practice for cruisers to be guided in by the marina manager.

The Bay Islands of Honduras are a very special destination. Promoted as a diving haven it is known as one of the best in the world. However, the resorts are fairly basic, and cater specifically for the diving fraternity, novices and experts alike. The largest fish in existence, the whale shark (which can get to 40 ft) is often spotted here. It is also an idyllic cruising ground with many sheltered bays behind its reefs.

Although it is part of Spanish-speaking Honduras, English is the preferred language for the majority of the locals (due to the British using the island for relocating the troublesome slaves of St Vincent and Jamaica).

It is a very laid-back place and when we try to check in we find that the port captain is away for a week and so the immigration office is closed. No one has a clue what to do so we just smile and carry on.

Lighthouse Reef, Belize

West End, on the northwestern corner, is protected by a low reef and here we find a diving and snorkelling mecca. So what makes it so good apart from the green crystal-like waters? Well, the topography is really interesting with its sheer drops, veins of lava covered in coral, and there are lots of healthy swarming fish. There is no current to speak of and even though it's deep we can see very clearly.

Belize

From West End on Roatan, Honduras, to the outer atolls of Belize, we have a perfect 80-nautical-mile daylight sail and en route manage to hook two beautiful dorado. As provisions have not been easy to come by, over recent weeks we have become hunters rather than gatherers.

We arrive with the sun behind us, so entering the outermost atoll requires a bow watch to negotiate the coral heads; I'm so nervous I can feel my T-shirt flapping against my belly. Lighthouse Reef Atoll is 40 nautical miles outside the Barrier Reef that borders Belize and its hundreds of cays. Here the cobalt-blue Caribbean Sea turns in an instant to turquoise blue over the sand. The depth and width through the breaking reef is only a matter of a few metres with clear visibility (almost too clear!) but once inside we weave our way to Half Moon Cay and anchor.

This is the perfect cay; a grove of coconut palms, a red-footed booby bird colony, white sand and 27°C waters that are perfect for snorkelling. Well, almost perfect. Just as we are about to jump from the dinghy in water that's only 1.5 metres deep, a 3-metre shark passes under us. Big and black, it's only a nurse shark but I've lived in Australia for too long to take sharks for granted so it stops me from getting wet. Ian ignores it and swimming around he is thrilled to find lobsters everywhere. Unfortunately they are out of season so we have to be content to just look at them.

In the middle of this 24-nautical-mile-long reef is the Blue Hole. Made world famous by Jacques Cousteau in 1972, it's a perfectly round and very deep hole with all the features of a cave including stalactites at 120 metres. Cousteau's discovery of the stalactites proved it was at one time above the water. The water is too shallow for us to cross the lagoon in our yacht so we hitch an early morning ride with the park rangers. It truly is a perfect deep blue circle, 150 metres across. We snorkel the rim with its covering of colourful ferns and coral and teeming with exotic fish, but I'm not in there long before a bluebottle jellyfish wraps its long trailing tentacles around my legs ... ouch! Ian has a great time practising his newfound but much loved hobby of underwater photography. We are content to snorkel rather than dive as a few divers, including one only three months ago, have been known never to return to the surface.

Through sparkling seas we meander from atoll to atoll, Lighthouse to Turneffe to Glover, until we enter the Barrier Reef that runs for a length of 190 nautical miles and is 15 nautical miles off the coast. It's the largest barrier reef in the western hemisphere, and second in the world to our Great Barrier Reef in Australia. Unique to it are the small islands on the edge of the reef. Saltwater Cay has a resort on the beach that's just 10 metres away from the sharply dropping reef. Guests can snorkel out the short distance to the edge of the reef and observe the sheer drop deep into the Caribbean Sea.

We meet Ray, a local, here with a group from the USA on a 'reefology' tour. When he learns we are from Australia he tells us the story of Steve Irwin's visit to their local crocodiles. Apparently Irwin hopped into the enclosure, as was his habit, and when the crocodiles chased him he hurdled the fence, saying afterwards, 'Crikey, they're more ferocious than ours!'

This is the season to visit the whale sharks that grow to over 14 metres long and which come every year to feed off the spawn of the snapper. We just miss seeing them as their visit is moon-dependent (up to 10 days past a full moon) and we are one day too late. Next time!

The Blue Hole, Half Moon Cay

Saltwater Cay on the Belize reef

Belize is a small enclave wedged between Mexico and Guatemala. Of no great interest to the Spanish during their quest for gold and silver in the early 1600s, it became a haunt for English pirates and subsequently became a British possession known as British Honduras. The official name of the territory was changed from British Honduras to Belize in June 1973 and full independence was granted in 1981. Unlike many other Central American countries – possibly due to its British heritage – it has had a very stable government. The English-speaking population of only 300,000 people is a mix of Kriol (i.e. Creole, a mix of European and African), Mestizo (European and Amerindian) and, of course, full-blooded Mayans.

The government has developed the country as an eco-friendly destination in the process preserving its national treasures. Over 45 per cent of the country has been declared a national park protecting the Mayan ruins, forest and especially the jaguars, large cats that still roam wild and were idolised in Mayan culture. The reef is similarly protected with many parks to preserve this beautiful region. Accommodation in the form of eco lodges can be found everywhere. It's hard to believe that we are still in the Caribbean; this area is generally known as either the northwest Caribbean or Continental Caribbean.

Turning south, we have to choose between so many cays to explore; some are covered in mangroves while others comprise just a circle of white sand dotted with coconut palms. We can't enter the Rio Dulce in Guatemala until 25 May because of a very shallow sandbar at its entrance that can only be crossed on a high spring tide, so we'll stay in Belize until then.

Placencia, a small village, is our main landfall and it is the base for Moorings, a boat chartering company that operates a large fleet of yachts. We highly recommend cruising Belize, especially in a catamaran. The general ambience is like being back in the eastern Caribbean with colourful Rastafarians, thatched-roof cottages and reggae music filling the bars at night. Nearby is the up-market resort of Turtle Inn, owned by Francis Ford Coppola (of *The Godfather* fame), which is run, along with a related operation in the mountains, as an eco resort.

The Sapodilla Cays are the most southerly islands on the barrier reef and it's very pleasant to spend our last days here in such idyllic surroundings. After seven months sailing 3200 nautical miles through the Caribbean Islands, with wonderful following winds, we are now motoring. It is steaming hot, there's no wind and the sea temperature is up to 28°C.

As we depart Belize for a new experience up the Rio Dulce in Guatemala, we are aware that we will be swapping turquoise seas for a huge freshwater river, sandy islands for a green jungle and colourful fish for monkeys – and maybe even a jaguar. But as the hurricane season approaches we need to move on and we know *Cape Finisterre* will be well protected in Guatemala.

Steaming hot Belize

Traditional Cayuca fishing on the Rio Dulce　　　*Texan Bay Lagoon, Rio Dulce*

Rio Dulce, Guatemala

Our entrance over the shallow sandbar into the Rio Dulce is unexpectedly dramatic and the captain's blood pressure rises. Twelve assorted yachts including us assume the spring high tide will give us enough water to cross, but three of us don't make it. Not an unusual happening as we are able to work out by the presence of a local fishing boat that's obviously standing by to come to the rescue, and which charges us plenty for the privilege. By hauling us over using a long halyard from the top of the mast, they are able to raise our keel just enough to skim the 200-metre length of the bar.

Livingston is our port of entry and six officials, wearing surgical masks in case we have swine flu, visit us on board before we are allowed ashore. The heat is extreme and we can't wait to sail up the winding river that flows beneath the mountains. As we enter the serene river

environment, the only thing we hear are cicadas and birds – no more wind whistling through the rigging. As the mountains close in behind us, we bid our farewell to the Caribbean Sea and soon we are dwarfed by a cascading jungle wall lush with growth. For the next 6 miles at every bend we see Mayans living at the river's edge and fishermen casting their nets from *cayucas* (canoes carved from logs) until we reach our first marina in an inlet surrounded by flowering white waterlilies and rushes.

The next day we take the dinghy up and down the small creeks that lead off the river. We see children paddling to and fro from school in their *cayucas*, we listen to monkey calls and we become avid bird watchers. Another 20 nautical miles up the river takes us to that section of the Rio Dulce where all the marinas are located. Hundreds of cruising yachts will spend the next six months here sheltering from the hurricane season.

Beautiful as it is we are mindful of security issues. Thefts from yachts in isolated anchorages do occur and someone was murdered on board their boat last year. For this reason it is wise not to anchor in the river and wherever you are you should always stay in the company of other yachts. All the marinas have security guards plus a patrol boat that cruises around at night, but despite these measures, an outboard was stolen from a yacht anchored beside us just off Mario's Marina.

What surprises us is the number of wealthy citizens of Guatemala City who have beautiful thatched-roof open-plan homes here where they keep their big powerboats on the river so they can access the Belize islands very quickly. After visiting two separate homes, one could almost be tempted to live here.

But what a small world it is; we strike up a conversation with one of the locals and when he asks if we know a guy in the South Island of New Zealand, it turns out that Ian went to school with him. (Maybe it's more that the South Island is small!)

We are leaving *Cape Finisterre* at RAM Marina for six months out of the water, but it's not quite out of the hurricane belt. However, as we're 26 nautical miles inland and behind a mountain range, we feel comfortable with our location – even if our insurance company isn't. Having said that, there was an earthquake last night that registered 7.1 on the Richter scale. Centred 250-nautical-miles away, it was enough to wake Ian making him think that someone had come alongside. But once he went up on deck and heard all the bird noise and dogs barking he realised it was the earth (and the river) moving. So much for coming inland, but at least we are safe from a possible tsunami out at sea.

The heat is exhausting and debilitating. We get up at 5 am, work until 9 and then hibernate in the air-conditioning until 4 pm. When the yacht is packed up, we decide to tour the Mayan ruins of Tikal for a few days. By bus we travel 300 km north through

Ian's Cruising Notes
HURRICANE SEASON

Summer in the Caribbean is hurricane season (1 June through to 30 November). Most insurance companies will insist that your yacht is moored either north of 35° or south of 12° in the northern hemisphere, which effectively means either sailing up the coast as far as Chesapeake Bay in North Carolina or south to Grenada or Trinidad. If the yacht is to be stored out of the water within these co-ordinates, it must be stored in a one-piece cradle. Alternatively, the props must be chained together on compacted ground and tied down at four corners to anchor points buried in the ground.

Last year we hauled out in Grenada and although a hurricane passed directly through the yard several years ago, this year they all formed well north and we weren't affected. No hurricane has ever reached *Cape Finisterre*'s current location out of the water in the Rio Dulce, Guatemala, although at 15° north, she is theoretically still in the hurricane zone. Other places where you can leave your yacht during the hurricane season include the Dutch ABC (Aruba, Bonaire and Curacao Islands just off the coast of Venezuela), and even Venezuela – although crime remains a concern there at present.

Back in Sydney, we track the hurricanes on www.buoyweather.com from the comfort of our home.

We prefer to haul our yacht out of the water in the off season and have done so for the last seven years – mainly because we are too far away to be able to do anything quickly should something go wrong while she is in the water.

All the yards are well set up with great security and at RAM Marina in Guatemala – where we've stored *Cape Finisterre* at the time of writing – we can actually see her via the web cam on their website. It's amazing being able to see the workers moving around and our boat cover moving in the breeze.

Regarding marine insurance providers, over time we have used two European-based companies: Pantaenius and Admiral. We are currently with Admiral as they were sponsors of the ARC and we've liked having personal contact with them. They handled our rig claim efficiently and professionally and we are also impressed with their extended cover for areas such as Cuba and hauling in Guatemala.

Rio Dulce river holiday house　　　　　　　*Ancient Mayan Temple, Tikal*

green cattle country. Our mission in visiting the temples of Indian Mayan civilisation is to try to understand the rise and fall of a great empire. Two thousand years ago, 10 million people lived in the area compared with the meagre population of 300,000 today. Howler and spider monkeys swing through canopies of tall trees, a habitat shared with exotically coloured birds such as the big-beaked toucan. Below, temples within recently cleared areas are visible after being lost to the jungle for centuries. What caused the demise of this civilisation? General opinion tends towards over-population in a barren area hastened by a prolonged drought (an early form of global warming) and of course, despite human sacrifices, the supposed failure of the gods to bring rain. Long thought to be peace-loving people, they are now recognised as being particularly warlike, which probably hastened their downfall.

The Mayans developed an advanced system of writing, mathematics and astronomy, which they used to calculate an accurate calendar that tracked a solar year of 365 days. The amazing thing is that they did this before the Europeans even began to understand astronomy and related matters. And without the use of the wheel or metal tools, they built enormous stone structures, a magnificent feat in itself.

Guatemala is a beautiful country with a total population of 12 million. Eighty per cent are Mayan Indian and the rest, of mainly Spanish origins, live in the capital, Guatemala City. At the time of the Spanish invasion in the sixteenth century, Central America was divided into departments with Guatemala the capital. The various departments make up the countries of the region as we know them today. For years run by the military, Guatemala is now enjoying a period of stability.

Ian's Cruising Notes
PASSAGE PLANNING AND SAFETY

It is important that all our voyages, whether just a day sail or over a longer period, are enjoyable and safe for both of us – and any guests on board – and to this end we always set ourselves up with a lifejacket, harness and a personal EPIRB (emergency position-indicating radio beacon) for signalling maritime distress.

For an overnight sail we check the weather for our planned days at sea and we arrange our departure at a time that ensures we will arrive at our destination in daylight hours, which sometimes means slowing down. Each time the life raft, man-overboard lights and sling get checked and then just before departing, we SMS (text) our son and daughter (Ian and Janey) with our trip details and an ETA so that in the event an EPIRB is activated, they will have full details for search and rescue. Ian and Janey are the primary contacts for our EPIRBs registered with AMSA in Australia.

All sailing manoeuvres and sail handling can be undertaken from the cockpit. If the wind is astern and we pole out the genoa wing and wing, the pole is set independently of the genoa using the topping lift, spinnaker downhaul and a brace aft to the winch. This way the genoa can be wound in and out, depending on the changing conditions, and in a man-overboard situation Andrea can roll it up quickly and easily. The mainsail has continuous reefing lines and can also be handled without going forward. The appropriate lines are all marked to the correct positions with fluoro thread sewn in.

At the navigation station, we have prominently displayed the radio emergency call procedure including the yacht's name, call sign and home port spelled phonetically.

YACHT NAME: CAPE FINISTERRE	CALL SIGN: VJN 2539	HOME PORT: SYDNEY
CHARLIE	VICTOR	SIERRA
ALFA	JULIET	YANKEE
PAPA	NOVEMBER	DELTA
ECHO		NOVEMBER
	TOO	ECHO
FOXTROT	FIFE	YANKEE
INDIA	TREE	
NOVEMBER	NINER	
INDIA		
SIERRA		
TANGO		
ECHO		
ROMEO		
ROMEO		
ECHO		

We have now extensively cruised both the
Mediterranean and the Caribbean and it is
interesting to note some of the similarities in
these two wonderful cruising grounds. For a start
they are almost identical in area: the Med being
842,125 sq nautical miles and the Caribbean
844,123. It is also worth noting that both have
very little tide. And most importantly each has

been a significant marine background to so many
major historical events.

So what were our lasting impressions? In a
coconut shell then, first and foremost we
remember the colours, and then the fantastic
sailing conditions, followed by how fit and
healthy we felt throughout.

Thank you for being with us all the way.

Acknowledgements

A big thank-you to the team at New Holland, particularly Belinda Cooke and Matt Turner, for making *Letters From the Med* such a success and believing I could do it again with *Letters from the Caribbean*. Thanks also to freelance editor Renée Lang and designer Trevor Newman.

Thanks to Janey and Ian for their patience – and for not letting us vegetate in our retirement.

And to all the friends who have joined and rejoined us many times; you have made our dream possible. Then there are all the people along the way whom we have met – from fellow cruisers to locals. We hope to cross paths with you again somewhere, sometime.

Our dream continues.

First published in 2010 by
New Holland Publishers (NZ) Ltd
Auckland · Sydney · London · Cape Town

www.newhollandpublishers.co.nz

218 Lake Road, Northcote, Auckland 0627, New Zealand
Unit 1, 66 Gibbes Street, Chatswood, NSW 2067, Australia
86–88 Edgware Road, London W2 2EA, United Kingdom
80 McKenzie Street, Cape Town 8001, South Africa

Publishing manager: Christine Thomson
Cover and text design: Trevor Newman
Project manager and editor: Renée Lang
Maps: Pauline Whimp

Printed in Singapore by Tien Wah Press (Pte) Ltd
Colour reproduction by Pica Digital Pte Ltd, Singapore

10 9 8 7 6 5 4 3 2 1

National Library of New Zealand Cataloguing-in-Publication Data

Treleaven, Andrea.
Letters from the Caribbean : sailing in the West Indies / Andrea and Ian Treleaven.
ISBN 978-1-86966-192-2
1. Treleaven, Andrea—Travel—Caribbean Sea. 2. Treleaven, Ian—Travel—Caribbean Sea. 3. Sailing—Caribbean Sea. 4. Caribbean Sea—Description and travel. I. Treleaven, Ian. II. Title.
910.916365—dc 22